BOOKS FOR SPECIAL DAYS

Integrated Teaching of Reading, Writing, Listening, Speaking, Viewing, and Thinking

JOYCE ARMSTRONG CARROLL

Illustrated by Leann Mullineaux

Jackdaws Series No. 4

1993
TEACHER IDEAS PRESS
A Division of
Libraries Unlimited, Inc.
Englewood, Colorado

Copyright © 1993 Libraries Unlimited, Inc.
All Rights Reserved
Printed in the United States of America

No part of this publication may be reproduced, stored in a retrieval system, or transmitted, in any form or by any means, electronic, mechanical, photocopying, recording, or otherwise, without the prior written permission of the publisher. An exception is made for individual library media specialists and teachers who may make copies of activity sheets for classroom use, in-service programs, or other educational programs in a single school.

TEACHER IDEAS PRESS
A Division of
Libraries Unlimited, Inc.
P.O. Box 6633
Englewood, CO 80155-6633

Library of Congress Cataloging-in-Publication Data

Carroll, Joyce Armstrong, 1937-
  Books for special days : integrated teaching of reading, writing, listening, speaking, viewing, and thinking / Joyce Armstrong Carroll ; illustrated by Leann Mullineaux.
    64 p. 22x28 cm. -- (Jackdaws series ; no. 4)
  Includes bibliographical references and index.
  ISBN 1-56308-077-X
  1. Language arts--United States--Handbooks, manuals, etc.
2. Children's literature--United States--Educational aspects--Handbooks, manuals, etc. 3. Holidays--Handbooks, manuals, etc.
4. Activity programs in education--United States--Handbooks, manuals, etc. I. Title. II. Series.
LB1576.C3172   1993
372.6'044--dc20   92-39403
                                                                CIP

INTRODUCTION

We all gathered around the birthday table, about 15 of us. I think I was six, but maybe it was my fifth birthday. Mom had set out all the usual party hats, cups, and plates. The cake—my favorite, chocolate with butter-cream icing—sat in the kitchen like a special guest waiting for a grand entrance.

Rita, Morry, and the rest capped their heads with the homemade paper hats Mom patiently sewed on her machine, and reached for the party favors. We all knew the routine—games, presents, then the party—first the hats, next the party favors, finally the singing of "Happy Birthday" to usher in the cake.

Surely Mom had made a mistake, for there were no party favors. All the kids looked at me; I looked at Mom, who began to smile as she got up, walked over to the closet, reached on tiptoe to the top shelf, and brought before us a huge crêpe-paper pie. "Little Jack Horner left this," she said. We squealed our delight. It looked just like a real pie. Then we noticed the ribbons peeking out from around the crust. Mom pulled each ribbon gently from the pie to each of us.

"We're not going to stick in our thumbs in this pie, but if each of you pull this ribbon, you'll pull out a plum of a surprise." We did.

Several years ago I met Theresa at a school reunion. Running back through life at school and in the old neighborhood like an old movie, she suddenly asked, "Do you remember that birthday when your mom made that fantastic pie with all the little surprises in it? I'll never forget that party. I still have mine—ran across it not too long ago."

Perhaps over the years that Little Jack Horner pie became mixed up in my mind with four-and-twenty blackbirds baked in a pie, the letter J for jackdaw from Edward Lear's *Nonsense ABCs*, and a bit of Piaget's concrete operational theory—but no matter—the concept of JACKDAWS was born.

Jackdaws are mischievous and curious birds that love to carry away and conceal small bright objects that attract their attention. Just as children love having a memento of a special day, they enjoy having a remembrance of a favorite story. I have found that integrating, writing, speaking, viewing, and thinking was easily accomplished through reading books and sharing keepsakes or "jackdaws."

On the following pages I share many jackdaws. Because it was difficult to designate an exact grade level, I have given a range of activities for most books. As you select your jackdaws, consider what will be appropriate for your participants, adapt the activities, and add your ideas to suit the needs of your students. Determine if students have allergies before serving food. You will find that as you share these books and activities, you and your students carry away many treasures, just like the curious jackdaw.

ACKNOWLEDGMENTS

This book would be like a one-layer, plain-vanilla cake if those listed below had not unselfishly brought icing, flavor, additional layers, decorations, and candles. To them, I am grateful.

Carol Lane, Alief ISD, for her "heart idea," which I used as the Valentine's Day integrated activity. **Richard Cohn**, Beyond Words Publishing, Inc., for sending me the beautiful book *The Great Change*. **Pam McDonald**, Pasadena ISD, for introducing me to Eric Kimmel. **Lee Jane Karlsson**, my assistant, for finding the badges and running the errands. **Phyllis Fees**, San Antonio ISD, for advice on mathematics, especially on the United Nations integrated activity. **Melissa Wendt**, *Neverending Tales*, for suggesting and finding many of the books. **Sharon Chamberlain**, Klein ISD, for Wilfrid Gordon. **Brenda Adcock and Debbie Kuczack**, *Imagination Station*, for *A B Cedar* and lots of other suggestions. *The Red Balloon* for *Appleblossom* and all the support of the folks there. **Pat Gray**, Texas Military Institute, for *Go In and Out the Window* and for truly sharing the music of books. **Coy L. Batson**, HBJ Publishers, for his generosity. **Lurlene Adams**, San Antonio ISD, for information on Kwanzaa. **Alana Morris**, Lewisville ISD, for having the common sense to tell me about Agatha. **Becky Ebner Hoag**, Northside ISD, for remembering my father with *My Father*. **Kelley Smith**, Spring ISD, for a plethora of ideas. **Joyce Harlow**, Summerfield Academy, for sharing information on early childhood. **Cindy Rogers**, Aldine ISD, for modeling the syllogistic thinking activity with James Stevenson's book. **Steve Bauer**, Pasadena ISD, for telling me about *Angel Child, Dragon Child*. **Mary Howard**, San Antonio ISD, for surprising me with *Ah!* **Eddie** for always being there.

Jackdaw 1

NAME TAGS

GENERAL SPECIAL DAYS
First Day of School

Title: *Annabelle Swift, Kindergartner*. Orchard Books, 1988.
Author: Amy Schwartz
Jackdaw: A name tag.
Summary: Lucy, a third grader, gives her sister Annabelle advice for her first day in school. Even though Lucy's advice does not always help, Annabelle has a successful day.

READING/WRITING CONNECTIONS

1. Provide students with blank name tags on which they write their names.
2. Ask students to share memories about their first day in school while wearing their name tags. Ask if any had an older brother or sister who gave them advice. Discuss.
3. Invite students to talk about what advice they would give a younger brother, sister, or friend about the first day of school. Talk about reasons for that advice.
4. Show the book's dust jacket. Students identify what they notice. Discuss the significance of the three milk cartons on the title page. Predict why they are there. Read the story.
5. Divide students into groups for dramatic play.
    a. Group one reenacts calling roll.
    b. Group two plays the colored lollipop game.
    c. Group three acts out recess.
    d. Group four does numbers on a felt board.
    e. Group five counts milk money (play money).

—EXTENSIONS—

LIBRARY CONNECTIONS

1. Share the acknowledgement with students. Discuss. Why might an author acknowledge a librarian?
2. Divide students into pairs. One student plays Lucy; the other plays Annabelle. They tell each other what happened the first time they visited a library.

INTEGRATED ACTIVITY

1. Annabelle loved to count. Divide students into groups. Give each group a freezer bag of pennies and nickels in play money. Groups count the money in the bags, give the total orally, and write the total in numbers or in words, or both.
2. Distribute paper on which you have drawn one milk carton. Using the milk as their focus, students write a word problem. They may include anything about the milk, its cost, the total number of cartons, and the number of straws or kindergartners getting milk, or both. Solve the problems together. Discuss.
3. Create other problems based on counting.

PUBLISHING

Let students decorate their name tags. Display on an I AM PROUD TO BE ME bulletin board.

Jackdaw 2

CROWNS

Birthdays

Title: *Happy Birthday, Ronald Morgan!* Puffin Books, 1986.
Author: Patricia Reilly Giff
Jackdaw: A gold paper crown.
Summary: Ronald has two problems: no school birthday and no best friend. It turns out that he is in for a surprise on both counts.

READING/WRITING CONNECTIONS

1. Show the cover. Invite students to make predictions about why Ronald Morgan looks the way he does. Ask students to identify the musical instrument on the dedication page. Discuss the illustration on the title page. Speculate on the time of year and how that might affect Ronald Morgan's birthday.
2. Read the story. Discuss birthdays in general, what happens, and why. Discuss feelings about birthdays. At appropriate times throughout the book, ask students how Ronald Morgan feels. Ask them to give reasons for their answers.
3. Ask how many students celebrate their birthdays during a school vacation. Explain that since some people have birthdays during school, whereas others have birthdays during school vacations, the class will participate in a birthday celebration for everyone.
4. Distribute gold paper and help students cut out crowns with points, like the one Miss Tyler made. They wear these crowns as they draw and write a birthday card for someone else in the class. (Draw names out of a hat.) Share.

—EXTENSIONS—

LIBRARY CONNECTIONS

1. When Ronald Morgan's class goes to the library, they tell stories. Invite students to tell stories about a birthday they remember or about some birthday they wish they had had. Share books that explore birthday observations in various cultures.
2. After the stories, Ronald Morgan visits the Quiet Corner. Show students how to locate the quiet area in the library. Talk about the purpose of the quiet area. Show students other sections of the library and explain the purposes of those sections. Discuss proper behavior in the quiet area and in other sections of the library.

INTEGRATED ACTIVITY

Help students make tambourines, using Margaret McLean's *Make Your Own Musical Instruments* (pp. 12-13) for step-by-step directions. Practice singing and playing the tambourines as preparation for accompaniment of a rendition of "Happy Birthday."

PUBLISHING

Display birthday cards on a HAPPY BIRTHDAY TO EVERYONE! bulletin board. Decorate the room with crêpe-paper streamers. Students sing and play "Happy Birthday." If possible, celebrate with lemon cookies and orange juice.

Jackdaw 3

BEACH SAND

Vacation Days

Title: *Moe the Dog in Tropical Paradise*. G. P. Putnam's Sons, 1992.

Author: Diane Stanley

Jackdaw: A tiny cup of beach sand.

Summary: Moe, disgruntled because of cold vacation weather, creates his own tropical paradise.

READING/WRITING CONNECTIONS

1. Write the word *vacation* on the board. Create a word map around the world. Use this map as a springboard for discussion of vacations, where people like to go, where people want to go, what vacations are for, spoiled vacations, best vacations, and so forth.
2. Show the book's cover. Invite comments about Moe's appearance. Based on his appearance, ask students to predict what might happen.
3. After reading the book, talk about the twist of Moe creating his own tropical paradise.
4. Distribute the beach sand. Invite students to use it as a prompt to write about a vacation they might create, just as Moe created his. (Have plenty of maps and globes available.) Share.

—EXTENSIONS—

LIBRARY CONNECTIONS

1. Divide students into groups according to designated countries. Each group studies its country and lists places in that country where people go for vacations and why those are good vacation spots. For example, in France: Paris, for its museums such as the Louvre; the French Riviera, for the Mediterranean; and so forth. (This can also be done with state and cities.) Students may use library resources, interviews, and local travel agencies. If time permits, they may write to consulates, chambers of commerce, and tourism facilities.
2. Arrange for students to present their findings to the class as if they were travel agents. They may wish to dress in the manner of their research, bring in artifacts, play music, or show art.

INTEGRATED ACTIVITY

Groups of students become marketing agents. Assign each group a well-known vacation spot, such as Disneyland or Hawaii. Establish the average tourist rate as 1,000 people per day. Each group's assignment is to increase tourism to the chosen spot by 25 percent. Remind them to create ways to persuade people to visit even if they have visited before. They could design brochures; do video spots, or create newspaper, magazine, or radio ads. After students investigate the ease of travel and the number of lodgings and restaurants in their group's area, they may write persuasive letters to those industries urging them to build more facilities to accommodate the expected increase. Calculate the profits to be made on this increase.

PUBLISHING

Create a butcher-paper banner reading "VACATION TIME!" Decorate the room with posters from travel agencies. Display all students' work.

Jackdaw 4

TOP HATS

JANUARY
New Year's Day
(January 1)

Title: *P. Bear's New Year's Party*. Beyond Words, 1989.
Author: Paul Owen Lewis
Jackdaw: A miniature top hat (available at craft stores).
Summary: P. (P for Polar) Bear invites his best-dressed friends to a New Year's party. They arrive in numerical order and in a time sequence from one to twelve.

READING/WRITING CONNECTIONS

1. Write *January* on the board. Tell students we call this month January because the Romans dedicated this month to Janus, who guarded their doors and the beginning of the year. Show pictures of Janus with two faces: one looking to the past, one looking to the future. In January, people still look back over the old year and forward to the new year when they make *resolutions* (promises to do better). Discuss these resolutions.
2. Put on a black top hat (available at party stores). Use as an introduction to the book and to formal attire. Talk about tuxedos and when they are worn. Show pictures (easily obtained from catalogs) of people in formal clothing.
3. After reading the book, talk about New Year's Eve and New Year's Day. Help students connect the idea of dressing formally and celebrating at parties as one way of welcoming the new year. Some students may know of other types of celebrations, such as New York's New Year's Eve Times Square celebration or the Philadelphia Mummer Parade. Share.
4. Distribute miniature top hats. Model how to draw a top hat. Students draw one, trace and cut out twelve, and use them for mathematics manipulatives.

—EXTENSIONS—

LIBRARY CONNECTIONS

1. Show a variety of invitations. Ask students to describe invitations they have received.
2. Make an enlarged blank invitation by folding an 18" x 12" piece of white paper in half, long side to long side. Model an invitation that encourages students to use the library. Include all necessary information inside and ask students to make suggestions for the outside of the invitation.
3. Distribute paper. Students fold the paper and write their own invitations. Share.

INTEGRATED ACTIVITY

Using the book, have students read the time on each clock and count the animals. Invite students to figure out how they can answer the last question in the book.

PUBLISHING

Make top hats out of cardboard. Students write the year on them and wear them home.

Jackdaw 5

STARS

Three Kings Day
(January 6: The Feast of the Epiphany)

Title: *Caspar and the Star*. Lion, 1991.

Author: Francesca Bosca (translated by Philip Hawthorn)

Jackdaw: A star.

Summary: Caspar of Tharsis, Melchior of Arabia, and Balthazar of Saba, having seen a new star which they believe means a great king is about to be born, follow it to Bethlehem. There they present gifts to the newborn baby and find a new joy in the King of Love.

READING/WRITING CONNECTIONS

1. Invite students to remember the names of the three kings. Write them in a circle on the board. Web that circle with all the things students can think of about these kings. Discuss.
2. After the reading, invite inferential thinking about how Caspar first became interested in stars. Talk about why people become interested in certain things. Discuss Caspar's motivation.
3. Examine Giuliano Ferri's illustrations of the star. Invite students to create their renditions of the star. Provide plenty of materials: sparkles, glue, paint, pastels, glitter, and multicolored, multitextured paper. Write stories or poems about the star. Display.

—EXTENSIONS—

LIBRARY CONNECTIONS

Have students work in small groups to research the following: the science of stars, use of stars for navigation, role of stars in literature, use of the word in our culture (star search, superstar, etc.), and so forth. Share findings.

INTEGRATED ACTIVITY

1. Ask students to lie down on the floor as if they were lying on a hill looking up at the sky. Connect this activity to looking at clouds. Talk about how we sometimes see shapes in clouds and then make up stories about those shapes. Explain that ancient peoples often looked at the stars, grouped them together, and created stories about them. Later, scientists invented telescopes that helped them study the stars. If possible, let students look through a telescope. Give the names and tell the stories of various stars. Explain how they are grouped into constellations such as the Big and Little Dippers.
2. Let each student choose a star or constellation and then write a story in which that star or constellation plays a major role. Distribute black paper and pins. Students carefully use the pins to punch out holes in the paper to represent stars for star maps.

PUBLISHING

After the students share their star maps and stories, hang them on windows in the classroom or school so the light shines through the holes.

Jackdaw 6

KEYS

Martin Luther King Jr. Day
(January 15: Celebrated on the third Monday in January)

Title: *This Is the Key to the Kingdom*. Little, Brown & Co., 1992.

Author: Diane Worfolk Allison

Jackdaw: A key (these may be real keys found at garage sales or flea markets or keys cut from heavyweight paper).

Summary: Through the illustrations to a classic nursery rhyme, a child finds a key and goes on a magical journey into a land filled with all that is noble, good, and beautiful.

READING/WRITING CONNECTIONS

1. Recite this well-known children's chant. Discuss possible meanings of *key* and *kingdom*. Show the dust jacket. Invite students to talk about what they see in the picture. Open to the title page. Discuss what the girl has been doing, where she lives, where she might be going, and what she sees. Ask students to predict what she might do next.
2. Look at the first page. Evaluate predictions. Discuss how the girl finds the key and predict what she will do next. Read through the book, taking time to show the rich illustrations.
3. Divide students into small groups. Ask groups to study the illustrations and list all the ideas of kingdoms suggested by the characters they can find. Share.
4. Distribute keys. Students write two things: the answer to the question posed at the end of the book and a description of their vision of the kingdom. Share.

—EXTENSIONS—

LIBRARY CONNECTIONS

Share information about Martin Luther King, Jr. Tell students that as a black minister from Atlanta, Georgia, Dr. King led a nonviolent struggle for racial equality in America. His method was passive resistance through boycotts, marches, and peaceful demonstrations. He was awarded the Nobel Peace Prize in 1964. Show students where they might find more information about Martin Luther King, Jr. Share all or excerpts from Dr. King's "I Have a Dream" speech.

INTEGRATED ACTIVITY

1. Play the recording of "We Shall Overcome" by Zilphia Horton, Frank Hamilton, Guy Carawan, and Pete Seeger, or show a documentary video such as *King: A Film Record*. Discuss.
2. After listening, viewing, and discussing, brainstorm ways this book works as a fitting tribute to King on his commemoration day. Draw from the students connections between the book and the goals of Dr. King.
3. In small groups, students construct posters that reflect the philosophy of Martin Luther King, Jr.

PUBLISHING

Display posters around the room. On the special day, everyone brings something they have written or read related to Martin Luther King, Jr. to share. Post on a bulletin board titled KEYS TO THE KINGDOM.

Jackdaw 7

POPCORN

National Nothing Day
(January 16)

Title: *Take Time to Relax!* Viking, 1991.
Author: Nancy Carlson
Jackdaw: Popcorn.
Summary: Tina and her family lived a hectic life. One day a snowstorm forced them into a "nothing" day, during which they discovered important things.

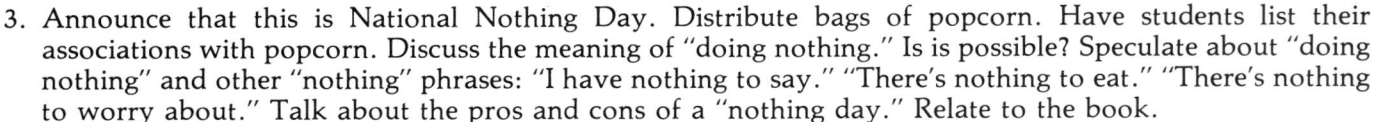

READING/WRITING CONNECTIONS

1. Ask students to write a schedule for a typical day in their life.
2. Ask students how the book cover makes them feel. Read the book and then create two word webs: one for a typical day in Tina's life, another for her "Nothing Day." Compare and contrast Tina's days. Compare and contrast with students' own schedules. Draw conclusions about the pace of life today.
3. Announce that this is National Nothing Day. Distribute bags of popcorn. Have students list their associations with popcorn. Discuss the meaning of "doing nothing." Is is possible? Speculate about "doing nothing" and other "nothing" phrases: "I have nothing to say." "There's nothing to eat." "There's nothing to worry about." Talk about the pros and cons of a "nothing day." Relate to the book.

—EXTENSIONS—

LIBRARY CONNECTIONS

Divide students into small groups. Challenge the groups to a "Nothing Scavenger Hunt." Each group finds as many connections to "nothing" as it can, using such library resources as thesauruses, dictionaries, encyclopedias, etymology books, books on quotations, mathematics texts, almanacs, and so forth. Share results.

INTEGRATED ACTIVITY

Divide students into pairs for the game "Zero Wins." The object of the game is to reach zero. If you get a negative number, you automatically lose. Designate one student **A**; the other **B**. Give each pair a calculator. (Adapted from Marilyn Burns's *Math for Smarty Pants*.)

1. **A** punches in a seven-digit number.
2. **B** chooses one of the numerals showing and punches it in, repeating it as many times as he or she wants, to make a number to subtract from the number shown.
3. After subtracting **B**'s number from the starting number, **A** chooses any numeral showing from the new number and does the same.
4. They continue doing this, taking turns.
5. The player who gets zero on the calculator first wins.

PUBLISHING

Fill a bulletin board with zeros of all sizes and colors. Students put some fact, problem, ideas, theory, saying, or something they have researched about "nothing" in the zeros. Title the board "Nothing to It!"

Jackdaw 8

FEATHERS

Common Sense Day
(January 29)

Title: *Agatha's Feather Bed: Not Just Another Wild Goose Story*. Peachtree, 1991.
Author: Carmen Agra Deedy
Jackdaw: A feather.
Summary: Agatha uses common sense when six angry geese come to reclaim their feathers.

READING/WRITING CONNECTIONS

1. Distribute feathers. Divide students into groups. Assign a scribe. Ask students to list as many purposes for feathers as they can. Share.
2. Show the cover of the book. Explain to students that although this story tells about common sense, it does other things too. Ask students to listen for idioms and to look closely at the items pictured in the borders.
3. Read the story. Stop for predictions at appropriate places.
4. Brainstorm as many puns, idioms, and word plays as students remember. Reread to check.
5. Write the poem Agatha tells all her customers on a chart. (Use later on bulletin board.) Invite students to recite it with you. Discuss its common sense. Discuss how Agatha uses common sense to solve her problem. Elicit a working definition for *common sense*.

—EXTENSIONS—

LIBRARY CONNECTIONS

Extend the idioms in the book by challenging students to research the meaning of the following list of idioms and write a common-sense sequel to Agatha's story using some or all of them.

a sitting duck	a lame duck	a dead duck
like water off a duck's back	swan song	proud as a peacock
wise as an owl	eagle eye	took to it like a duck to water
feather in one's cap	make the feathers fly	bird's-eye view
in fine feather	featherweight	Mother Goose
to smooth ruffled feathers	to feather one's own nest	birds of a feather flock together

INTEGRATED ACTIVITY

1. Divide students into pairs. As partners they generate a list of questions about something mentioned in the book, for example "boar-bristle brush." They decide on three good questions from their lists, which they exchange with another pair.
2. The second pair researches that item and then writes out the answers to the questions they were given.

PUBLISHING

Display answers around Agatha's poem. Title it EVERYTHING COMES FROM SOMETHING!

JACKDAW 8—Copyright 1992 Teacher Ideas Press, a division of Libraries Unlimited, Inc., P.O. Box 6633, Englewood, CO 80155-6633

Jackdaw 9

FORTUNE COOKIES

JANUARY/FEBRUARY
Chinese New Year
(The second new moon after the first day of winter)

Title: *Why Rat Comes First: A Story of the Chinese Zodiac.* Children's Book Press, 1991.

Author: Retold by Clara Yen

Jackdaw: A Chinese fortune cookie.

Summary: This book recounts one fictionalized reason why the Chinese calendar is arranged as it is.

READING/WRITING CONNECTIONS

1. Read "About the Story" in the back of the book. Discuss this book as a work of fiction. Read about the author and the illustrator.
2. After reading the story, encourage students to check the year of their birth and see what animal sign they fall under according to the Chinese zodiac cycle. Discuss. Emphasize this as fiction, but also use it to explain why the Chinese consider this day everyone's birthday.
3. Distribute Chinese fortune cookies. Discuss why these are another type of fiction. Students read their fortunes and then share them with a partner, discussing whether their fortunes fit their animal signs.
4. Distribute tiny slips of paper. Using sources such as Bartlett's *Familiar Quotations*, each person finds a quotation to write for his or her partner. Share.

—EXTENSIONS—

LIBRARY CONNECTIONS

Show students a picture of a traditional zodiac. Invite comments. Read the dictionary definition of the zodiac. Talk about why the constellations are so named and so divided. Discuss. Ask students to conjecture about time, dividing time, and needing a calendar.

INTEGRATED ACTIVITY

Divide students into pairs. Partners design a calendar for people to use in today's world. As models, in addition to the Chinese calendar, students research different calendars, such as the Aztec calendar, the Gregorian calendar, the Jewish calendar, and the Julian calendar. Calendars should include:

1. A description of how the reckoning system was devised
2. The length and divisions of the calendar
3. Names for the divisions (for example, the Chinese call months "moons," as do the Native Americans)
4. An explanation or rationale for the calendar's design and a sample.

Younger children could choose and fill in special days on a preprinted calendar of the upcoming month.

PUBLISHING

Partners share their calendars. Display work on a bulletin board, AS THE WORLD TURNS.

JACKDAW 9—Copyright 1992 Teacher Ideas Press, a division of Libraries Unlimited, Inc., P.O. Box 6633, Englewood, CO 80155-6633

Jackdaw 10

SONGBOOKS

FEBRUARY
National Music Month

Title: *Go In and Out the Window*. Henry Holt & Co., 1987.

Authors: Dan Fox (arranged and edited the music) and Claude Marks (wrote the commentary)

Jackdaw: A songbook.

Summary: Sixty-one traditional childhood songs are illustrated with photographs of items from the Metropolitan Museum of Art. Each song is accompanied by a discussion of both the music and the art with a fingering chart for chords.

READING/WRITING CONNECTIONS

1. Explain that February is National Music Month. Show the book and see if student recognize the allusion in the title. Sing the song together.
2. Open to the song in the book and show the picture. Ask students if they can figure out in what country this house might be. Look for hints in the picture.
3. The commentary describes this as a ditty. Look up *ditty* in the dictionary.
4. Form a circle and count off. Half the students join hands and hold them above their heads. The other half join hands and "go in and out the window" by moving under the hands and around the backs of those forming a circle. Reverse the groups. Discuss this activity. With older students, ask if they remember this activity or other activities associated with the music.
5. Divide students into groups to compose additional verses for the song, such as "Go in and out the mall's stores," or "Go in and out the principal's office." Share.
6. These verses might constitute a group's entire songbook, or they might be the first entry in students' songbooks. Creating new verses could be an ongoing project throughout the month.

—EXTENSIONS—

LIBRARY CONNECTIONS

Continue working on music throughout the month. Students may add to their songbooks.

INTEGRATED ACTIVITY

Bring in catalogs and old magazines. Students cull pictures to accompany the songs in their songbooks. They arrange the art and write a brief commentary on the art and music. Students may add covers.

PUBLISHING

Display students' songbooks beside books on music and art. Call the display OF THEE I SING!

Jackdaw 11

CALENDARS

Groundhog Day
(February 2)

Title: *It's Groundhog Day!* Scholastic, 1987.

Author: Steven Kroll

Jackdaw: A calendar (these may be old calendars, photocopies, or advertising calendars).

Summary: As Godfrey Groundhog prepares for hibernation, he speculates that he may not see his shadow when he emerges. This dismays Roland Raccoon, who wants a long winter in his ski lodge.

READING/WRITING CONNECTIONS

1. Take students to a window. Ask them what kind of day it is. Ask if they think the groundhog saw his shadow. Talk about what people say happens when the groundhog sees or does not see his shadow. Go outside and let students look for their shadows. Talk about what makes a shadow. Tell students that when they return to the room, you will read a story about this day.
2. Before reading, explain that *groundhog* is another name for woodchuck, given by early New England settlers, who called this animal *groundhog* after the hedgehog they remembered from England. Show students several pictures of real groundhogs.
3. After reading and discussing the story, distribute the calendars. Tell students to listen carefully as you reread the section up until Godfrey goes to sleep. Ask students to circle in crayon the month and the day they think Godfrey went into his burrow.
4. Share the student's circled guesses and let them tell why they made their choices. Using the book, examine clues in the words and pictures that help the reader know the time of year. Talk about how important words and pictures are to understanding. Talk about the importance of listening. Talk about estimating and how students chose the day to circle. Use your own calendar as a model.
5. Conclude by inviting students to identify February 2 and circle it in another color.

—EXTENSIONS—

LIBRARY CONNECTIONS

Gather nonfiction books about animals that live underground. Compare the facts with the portrayals of the same animals in the book. Challenge the students to identify discrepancies, misleading information, etc. Discuss how authors use information for inspiration as they write.

INTEGRATED ACTIVITY

Distribute round boxes (oatmeal) or round paper tubes from which students may make burrows. After painting the burrows with brown tempera, students construct burrow doorways from brown clay and straw. Then each writes a story about the groundhog in his or her burrow.

PUBLISHING

Display the calendars, burrows, students' stories and pictures, and the book.

JACKDAW 11—Copyright 1992 Teacher Ideas Press, a division of Libraries Unlimited, Inc., P.O. Box 6633, Englewood, CO 80155-6633

Jackdaw 12

TOOTHBRUSH WANDS

Dental Health Week
(February: First week)

Title: *The Real Tooth Fairy*. Harcourt Brace Jovanovich, 1990.

Author: Marilyn Kaye

Jackdaw: A toothbrush "wand" (decorated with a star garland).

Summary: Elise loses a tooth but finds the real tooth fairy.

READING/WRITING CONNECTIONS

1. Tell children this is Dental Health Week. Encourage students who have lost teeth to tell how many they have lost, when they lost them, and what they did with those teeth. Talk about the tooth fairy.
2. Read the book and discuss.
3. Distribute star garlands and toothbrushes. Students wind the garland around the brushes to make a toothbrush wand. Then they write story about a tooth fairy. Share.

—EXTENSIONS—

LIBRARY CONNECTIONS

1. Obtain some outdated tooth x-rays from a local dentist. Hold them up to a window so students can see the insides of the teeth. This helps them better understand why teeth and gums have to be properly cared for. (See "Health/Science/Mathematics Connections" in Carroll's *Story Books*, Jackdaw 10.) Research the science or health sections in the library for books about x-ray technology, pictures of x-rays, who invented x-rays, and why they are taken.
2. Show a collection of teeth. (A taxidermist, veterinarian, or zoo keeper could help. Often rock shops have fossilized teeth.) Let children compare these to their own teeth. If possible, show a set of false teeth. After exploring the information in library books on teeth, students find their incisors, cuspids, bicuspids, and molars. Students look in the mirror and draw themselves with missing teeth. Display pictures.

INTEGRATED ACTIVITY

1. Give each student pink modeling clay. Students mold the clay into two horseshoe-shaped "gums" (about 3" x 3"). Students press small pasta tubes (open side down) into the lower "gum," starting in the front middle, so that there are eight "teeth" on each side. They do the same with the upper gum, trying to get the teeth to match up with the bottom teeth for a good bite. Put the gums together.
2. Students count how many teeth they have in their model jaws.
3. Students point out the incisors, cuspids, bicuspids, and molars.
4. Using their model jaws and their toothbrush wands, students dramatize brushing their teeth and massaging their gums.

PUBLISHING

Create a display called JAWS THIRTY-TWO. Write the title in thick white paint to approximate toothpaste. Arrange books, students' stories, pictures, and jaws around a picture of a shark or poster from the film *Jaws*.

Jackdaw 13

INVENTIONS

National New Ideas Week
(February: The second week)

Title: *A Bicycle for Rosaura*. Kane/Miller, 1991.

Author: Daniel Barbot

Jackdaw: An invention.

Summary: Rosaura, a handsome hen, has a new idea. She requests a bicycle for her birthday. Señora Amelia tries to fulfill Rosaura's birthday wish.

READING/WRITING CONNECTIONS

1. Show students an ordinary item, anything from a needle to a wristwatch. Lead students by a series of questions to see that someone had to come up with the idea for this item. When they do, we call them inventors. When they uncover a new idea, we call them discoverers. Sometimes, when people come up with new ideas about life, we call them philosophers. Sometimes when someone comes up with a new idea, people say the person is crazy, unrealistic, or a dreamer. Discuss what makes the difference.

2. Divide students into groups. Assign each group the task of telling how to make one of the things the strange-looking man said he could make: rollerskates for dogs, eyeglasses for cats, a singing spoon, a chocolate rocking chair. Share.

—EXTENSIONS—

LIBRARY CONNECTIONS

1. Show Saul Bass's film *Why Man Creates* (25 min., color). After viewing and discussing the film, divide students into groups. Group I writes all the unusual examples of creativity in their town or city (e.g., architecture, window displays); Group II records the best movies they have seen lately and the movies' creative elements; Group III generates a list of creative people and tells why they are considered creative; Group IV chooses a common item from the classroom and creates a new use for it. Share. Discuss why some people achieve their creative potential while others do not. (This activity can be done even if students do not see the film.)

2. Consult Jerry D. Flack's book *Inventing, Inventions, and Inventors* for ideas, from games to biographies and from creative thinking exercises to a rubric for inventing.

INTEGRATED ACTIVITY

Tell students that sometimes new ideas start by looking at one thing and seeing another. H. C. Booth looked at the wind, reversed it, and came up with the vacuum cleaner. Newton saw the connection between the apple falling and the moon setting, which led to the theory of gravity. After this introduction, have students pick two items from a miscellaneous items bag. They find a connection between the two objects or a new purpose for the objects. They may do what the strange-looking man in the book did—jot down numbers and work complicated formulas—or they may "invent" in their own fashion.

PUBLISHING

Display students' new ideas under a NEW IDEAS banner. Share and discuss.

Jackdaw 14

VALENTINES

Valentine's Day
(February 14)

Title: *Somebody Loves You, Mr. Hatch*. Bradbury Press, 1991.
Author: Eileen Spinelli
Jackdaw: A replica of an antique valentine.
Summary: Reclusive Mr. Hatch receives an anonymous valentine, which changes his life. Realizing it was delivered to him by mistake, Mr. Hatch begins to resume his old ways, but his neighbors and friends have other ideas.

READING/WRITING CONNECTIONS
1. Write "Somebody loves you." on board or chart. Brainstorm the feelings that sentence evokes. Ask students how they would feel if they received an anonymous valentine. Discuss.
2. Introduce the book by explaining this is what happened to Mr. Hatch.
3. After the story, divide students into small groups. Each group lists names of specific people who would not expect to receive a valentine from them, such as the lady in the cafeteria, a senior citizen who lives down the street, a distant cousin. Students circle one person on the list they might surprise with a valentine card.
4. Students replicate antique cards by using paper doilies in silver, white, and gold, as well as ribbons and dried flowers. Their cards may open like fans, pop up, or have moveable flaps.

—EXTENSIONS—

LIBRARY CONNECTIONS
1. Show students how to locate addresses in a telephone book. Demonstrate how to alphabetize to the second and third letter. Show students how to locate the Zip Code.
2. Practice addressing envelopes.

INTEGRATED ACTIVITY
1. Distribute five three-inch hearts: one red, two purple, and two pink.
2. Read the following word problem (this may be reworded to fit different grade levels): "Maria wanted to see if Jesse could build a heart totem pole using five hearts and five clues. Jesse did. Can you? Here are the clues: a. No hearts of the same color are next to each other. b. The top heart is not pink. c. The heart in the center is not red. d. One pink heart is just below a red one. e. The bottom heart is not pink."
3. Work this problem on the overhead along with students. Divide students into small groups. Distribute several white paper hearts to each group. Each group formulates a design using the hearts, decides on metaphoric language for that design (e.g., "moon-shaped" instead of "round"), and writes clues for others to try to recreate the design.
4. Exchange clues. Groups work out the designs according to the clues. Check.
5. Discuss what was learned from this activity.

PUBLISHING
Affix designs and clues on cardboard for a HEARTS TO YOU! bulletin board display.

JACKDAW 14—Copyright 1992 Teacher Ideas Press, a division of Libraries Unlimited, Inc., P.O. Box 6633, Englewood, CO 80155-6633

Jackdaw 15

CAMPAIGN BUTTONS

Presidents' Day
(February: Third Monday)

Title: *The Buck Stops Here: The Presidents of the United States*. Harper & Row, 1990.

Author: Alice Provensen

Jackdaw: A cardboard campaign button.

Summary: Rhyming couplets, detailed pictures, symbols, and historical facts capture the essence of each president from Washington to Bush. A "Notes About the Presidents" section at the end of the book furnishes additional information, and there is a "Selected Bibliography."

READING/WRITING CONNECTIONS

1. Write the expression "The Buck Stops Here" on the board. Ask students if they know who made that phrase famous, what it means, and why it was coined. (See information on Truman in "Notes.")
2. Show the dust jacket. Cover the names and challenge students to identify as many of the pictured presidents as possible. Discuss the pictures of the White House, the eagle, and the helicopter. Continue this same procedure as you examine the details on the title page.
3. Read the introduction and the pages about Washington and Lincoln.
4. Distribute cardboard. Working in groups, students design campaign buttons for either Washington or Lincoln based on the information given on those presidents' pages. Share buttons.

—EXTENSIONS—

LIBRARY CONNECTIONS

1. Help students understand the functions of the additional sections of the book.
2. Choose one of the presidents. Locate all the books and material in the library related to that president. Lead students to see the magnitude of information available. Discuss the process of synthesizing that Provensen might have used when choosing what would be in the book. Relate this to any research process.

INTEGRATED ACTIVITY

1. Read *The Go-Around Dollar* by Barbara Johnston Adams. Point out all the research that went into writing this book.
2. Students choose another denomination and research the president who appears on that bill. For information on which president's portrait appears on which bill and other facts about U.S. currency, they may send a postcard to: Publications Department, Federal Reserve Bank of Boston, 600 Atlantic Avenue T-6, Boston, MA 02106. Ask for "Dollar Points."
3. Use *The Go-Around Dollar* as a model for writing up students' own research.

PUBLISHING

Together, create a BUCK STOPS HERE display of books and research.

JACKDAW 15—Copyright 1992 Teacher Ideas Press, a division of Libraries Unlimited, Inc., P.O. Box 6633, Englewood, CO 80155-6633

Jackdaw 16

POTATO CHIPS

MARCH
St. Patrick's Day
(March 17)

Title: *Jamie O'Rourke and the Big Potato*. G. P. Putnam's Sons, 1992.

Author: Tomie dePaola

Jackdaw: Natural potato chips.

Summary: Jamie O'Rourke catches a leprechaun, who gives him one potato seed instead of a pot of gold.

READING/WRITING CONNECTIONS

1. Bring in the biggest old potato you can find, one with "eyes." Show it to the students. Discuss how it grows, how it was harvested, its origins, where it grows, ways to eat potatoes, its buds or "eyes," slang words for potatoes (e.g., spud), and the idiom "hot potato."
2. Distribute chips before reading the story. Connect potatoes, the Irish, St. Patrick's Day, and the telling of folktales before you begin. Read "A Note About the Story."
3. After reading, "What to do now?," pause and ask students what they think Jamie and the villagers will do. Help students investigate all the possibilities.
4. Stop after "I saved a potato eye for a seed and it's just about time to plant it." Invite students to write their own endings to the story. Share.
5. Read dePaola's ending. Discuss how the endings are alike and different.

—EXTENSIONS—

LIBRARY CONNECTIONS

1. (Grades Pre-K—2) Teach the children's chant "One Potato, Two Potato." Divide students into small circles and let them say the chant and count off as a game.
2. (Grades 3-5) Divide students into teams to: research all the vegetables that are in the same nightshade family as the potato; compile a list of vegetables that are grown underground; draw a map of Ireland and label some of its cities; read about St. Patrick; find facts about the Great Potato Famine (1845 to 1849). Share research.

INTEGRATED ACTIVITY

Bring in potatoes and allow each student to pick one. Tell them to examine it carefully, so carefully that they would be able to identify it among other potatoes. Collect all potatoes and mix them up. Students try to find their potatoes. Those who do tell how they distinguished theirs from the others. Those who could not find theirs speculate why not. Brainstorm ways people remember things (e.g., marking, labeling, writing the name on an item, memorizing a rhyme, etc.) and write descriptions.

PUBLISHING

Students sit in a circle and each introduces his or her potato person. Then each student reads his or her description. Display potato people and descriptions in an exhibit entitled SPUDS.

JACKDAW 16—Copyright 1992 Teacher Ideas Press, a division of Libraries Unlimited, Inc., P.O. Box 6633, Englewood, CO 80155-6633

Jackdaw 17

TWIGS

National Wildlife Week
(March: Begins on the third Sunday)

Title: *Were You a Wild Duck, Where Would You Go?* Stewart, Tabori & Chang, 1990.

Author: George Mendoza

Jackdaw: A twig.

Summary: As a wild duck searches through its polluted environment for a home, it thinks of an earlier, bountiful time and encourages restoration of the environment.

READING/WRITING CONNECTIONS

1. Read the first page and talk about its meaning.
2. After reading the book, divide students into groups. Distribute twigs. Students generate ideas that connect the book and the twigs. Share. Inform students that this is National Wildlife Week, a time to think about the various forms of wildlife in our world.
3. Discuss criteria for categorizing "wildlife." Students then generate a list of all the wildlife they know. Share.

—EXTENSIONS—

LIBRARY CONNECTIONS

1. Write a postcard to The National Wildlife Federation, 1412 16th Street, N.W., Washington, DC 20036, requesting #79301, "Backyard Wildlife Kit."
2. Choose one of the following organizations to which to write a letter, requesting information about wildlife:
   Animal Welfare Institute, P.O. Box 3650, Washington, DC 20007
   National Audubon Society, 950 Third Avenue, New York, NY 10022
   Greenpeace, USA, P.O. Box 4739, Santa Barbara, CA 93103
   The Humane Society of the United States, 2100 L Street, N.W., Washington, DC 20037.
3. Together use the information from these groups, augmented by library research, as the basis to create a school banner for National Wildlife Week.

INTEGRATED ACTIVITY

Divide students into three large groups. Each group plans a method of presenting its work.

1. Group I researches endangered animals: gorillas; elephants; orangutans; wooly spider monkey; Australian ghost bat; Grevy's zebras; African wild ass; Estuarine crocodile; tigers.
2. Group II researches exotic animals from tropical rain forests: coatimundis; jaguars; anteaters; tamarins; kinkajous; sylphs; ocelots; hoatzins; tapirs; sloths; tree frogs; tree boas.
3. Group III researches Jane Goodall's 30 years of work in Africa.

PUBLISHING

Wildlife Week! Groups share research through pictures, dramatizations, and music.

Jackdaw 18

CLICKERS

Spring Equinox
(March 21 or 22)

Title: *The Animal That Drank Up Sound.* Harcourt Brace Jovanovich, 1992.

Author: William Stafford

Jackdaw: A clicker (metal or plastic—the metal ones are louder).

Summary: An enormous animal drinks up all sound on earth, leaving it cold and frozen. A little cricket ushers in the return of spring with a simple, "Cricket."

READING/WRITING CONNECTIONS

1. Write this quotation from Henry Van Dyke on the board or chart: "The first day of spring in one thing, and the first spring day is another. The difference between them is sometimes as great as a month." Discuss. Talk about what makes spring.
2. Distribute clickers to students. Invite them to participate by providing background sound. Designate one student to click at a given signal. Ask the others to use their clickers when you give the group a signal to begin and to stop. Practice the signals and clicks without the book.
3. Turn off the lights. Begin reading in a soft whisper. As you read the word "Cricket!," signal the single student. As you begin "It all returned," give the group signal to begin. After "any time," signal to stop. Finally, signal the single student to click during "and practices at night."
4. Read the book through without background sound and in your normal speaking voice.
5. Distribute index cards. On them, students write which way they preferred the reading and why.
6. Students tape their cards in the appropriate column on a large sheet of butcher paper that has been prepared with the following headings and then discuss results.

The Animal That Drank Up Sound

With accompaniment   Without accompaniment

—EXTENSIONS—

LIBRARY CONNECTIONS

Remind students that today is the spring equinox, sometimes called the *vernal* equinox. Today there will be 12 hours of night and 12 hours of day. Research why there are time zones and daylight savings.

INTEGRATED ACTIVITY

Debra Frasier, the illustrator, tells how she created the art collages for this book in "Note from the Author and Illustrator." Challenge students to replicate the process as a background for their own writings. They make some preliminary sketches and then follow Frasier's directions.

PUBLISHING

Mount students' work on a bulletin board titled SPRING IS A CALL TO ACTION.

JACKDAW 18—Copyright 1992 Teacher Ideas Press, a division of Libraries Unlimited, Inc., P.O. Box 6633, Englewood, CO 80155-6633

Jackdaw 19

EGGS

MARCH/APRIL
Easter
(The Sunday after the first full moon on or following the vernal equinox)

Title: *Rechenka's Eggs*. Philomel Books, 1988. (International Reading Association Award)

Author: Patricia Polacco

Jackdaw: A hard-boiled egg.

Summary: Old Babushka always wins the Moskva Easter Festival with her beautifully painted eggs. One day she takes in an injured goose, which she names Rechenka, who accidentally breaks all of Babushka's eggs. Rechenka repays Babushka for her kindness with several surprises.

READING/WRITING CONNECTIONS

1. Distribute eggs. Students hold the eggs during the reading. Then ask students what they think they will do with the eggs. Accept all answers. (Most will suggest a variation of coloring or decorating the egg.) Then challenge students to stand their eggs on end. Provide ample time and give no hints. (They must crush its tip.) Discuss implications for all types of problem solving.

2. Divide students into three groups for further problem solving. Group one polls 25 people about their egg-eating preferences and grids the results. Group two constructs a paper metric tape, measures ten eggs from end to end, and grids the results. Group three writes out possible solutions to the following problem: If you are standing on concrete, how could you drop a raw egg four feet without breaking the shell and without using anything to cushion the fall? (Drop it from five feet and it will drop four feet without breaking.) Groups share.

—EXTENSIONS—

LIBRARY CONNECTIONS

Divide students into teams. Ask them to find the meanings of egg idioms, such as "egg on one's face," "an egg head," "a bad egg," "walk on eggshells," "as sure as eggs is eggs," "don't put all your eggs in one basket," "you can't make an omelette without breaking eggs," "to over egg the cake," "to unscramble," "I have eggs on the spit," "like two eggs," "to egg on," "to take eggs for money," and "There is reason in roasting egg."

INTEGRATED ACTIVITY

1. Challenge students to design and build a container for a raw egg that will protect the egg from breaking when dropped from the top floor of the school.

2. Make sure students keep a log of their processes, from their initial idea or ideas, through their design or designs, to the tests, trials and errors, the final test, results, and conclusions.

PUBLISHING

On EGG DROP DAY, students test their containers. Successful students are not "rotten eggs."

JACKDAW 19—Copyright 1992 Teacher Ideas Press, a division of Libraries Unlimited, Inc., P.O. Box 6633, Englewood, CO 80155-6633

Jackdaw 20

APPLE BLOSSOMS

Passover
(Eight days beginning the fifteenth day of the Hebrew month Nisan)

Title: *Appleblossom*. Harcourt Brace Jovanovich, 1991.

Author: Shulamith Levey Oppenheim

Jackdaw: An apple blossom (real, dried, faux).

Summary: Naphtali uses the traditional ritual at the Passover Seder to convince his father to let him keep Appleblossom, a talking cat.

READING/WRITING CONNECTIONS

1. Write the Hebrew word *Pesach* on the board. Tell students it means "pass over" and refers to the eight days beginning on the fifteenth day of the Hebrew month Nisan. It marks the anniversary of the passage of the angel of death, who killed the first-born children of the Egyptians but passed over the houses of the children of Israel that had been marked by the blood of lambs.

2. Invite students to contribute what they know about the Passover holiday. Discuss the ceremonial meal, the Seder, the Haggadah, and the liturgy book.

3. Introduce the book by showing the picture of Naphtali and Appleblossom opposite the title page. Read the introductory note. Invite speculation about what might happen in this book.

4. After reading to page 17, distribute the apple blossoms. Divide students into groups and have each group select a scribe. Each group writes its prediction of Appleblossom's plan. Share. Finish reading the book. Discuss how closely the groups' plans matched Appleblossom's. Discuss what Appleblossom needed to know for his plan. Discuss what is needed for any plan to work.

—EXTENSIONS—

LIBRARY CONNECTIONS

1. Read the story of the Passover from the Old Testament's Book of Exodus. Discuss.

2. Show students where to find information in the library pertaining to the significance of the Seder foods, such as unleavened bread (matzo), gefilte fish, matzo ball soup, hareset, compote and macaroons, chopped liver, carrot tzimme, potato kugel, horseradish, knaidlach, kishka, potato knish, and apple schalet. Students may also research Orthodox Jewish dietary laws and customs and rabbinic supervision.

INTEGRATED ACTIVITY

1. The Torah contains the Five Books of Moses, which tell the story of the Jewish people and their laws and teachings. Suggest that students create stories based on their own study of Jewish traditions, to be written on Torah-like scrolls.

2. Divide students into small groups. Students research Jewish traditions and discuss possible stories to fit those traditions. They may use *Appleblossom* as a model. Distribute rolls of paper towels. After prewriting, writing, and editing their stories, students write them on their "scrolls."

PUBLISHING

Students gather together in a circle to share their scroll stories. Display after sharing.

JACKDAW 20—Copyright 1992 Teacher Ideas Press, a division of Libraries Unlimited, Inc., P.O. Box 6633, Englewood, CO 80155-6633

Jackdaw 21

TELESCOPES

APRIL
April Fool's Day
(April 1)

Title: *Arthur's April Fool*. Little, Brown & Co., 1983.
Author: Marc Brown
Jackdaw: A cardboard-tube telescope.
Summary: Binky threatens to ruin Arthur's tricks at the April Fool's Day assembly, but Arthur outsmarts him.

READING/WRITING CONNECTIONS

1. Talk about April Fool's Day and the meaning of the word *fool*. Elicit from students the kinds of tricks and pranks people play on this day. Explain that this is an old custom dating back to when April 1 marked the end of an eight-day New Year celebration. Some people kept that custom even after the calendar was changed and January 1 marked the New Year, so these people were called April's fools.
2. Show the cover of the book. Discuss what Arthur might be doing. Ask students to identify the clues that led them to their answers.
3. Talk about each of Arthur's friends pictured at the book's beginning. Ask the students to tell what is funny about each picture.
4. Read the book. This book lends itself to frequent discussion of sequence and predictions.
5. Give students two cardboard tubes, one shorter than the other. Students insert one into the other to resemble a telescope. They tape clear food wrap or contact paper over the ends. They paint and decorate their telescopes. Then they write descriptions of what they see through their telescopes. Share.

—EXTENSIONS—

LIBRARY CONNECTIONS

1. Share and display a corpus of work by the author. See Sharron L. McElmeel's *Bookpeople: A First Album* for a selected bibliography and a brief biography.
2. Share books on magic tricks and practice execution of some.
3. Students choose their favorite Brown book and do a book talk.

INTEGRATED ACTIVITY

1. Make a class April Fool's Animal Alphabet Book. Create the first page together with students so they can use it as a model. Because Arthur is an aardvark, begin with **A**ardvark.
2. Let students create other pages individually or in small groups. They write the name of the animal, use words starting with the same letter to describe the animal, include facts about the animal, draw the animal, and add anything else. The April Fool's trick is to hide something extra on the page for the reader to find. Students provide an answer key for the back of the book.

PUBLISHING

Hold a "Find What's Hidden Huddle." Students form a group huddle, exchange animal alphabet pages, and search for the hidden extras. Bind and display the finished alphabet book.

JACKDAW 21—Copyright 1992 Teacher Ideas Press, a division of Libraries Unlimited, Inc., P.O. Box 6633, Englewood, CO 80155-6633

Jackdaw 22 — STORY CLOTHS

International Children's Book Day
(Hans Christian Andersen's Birthday—April 2)

Title: *Nine-In-One, Grr! Grr!* Children's Book Press, 1989.
Author: Blia Xiong (adapted by Cathy Spagnoli)
Jackdaw: A story cloth.
Summary: Shao promises Tiger nine cubs every year if Tiger remembers the words. Bird tricks Tiger to prevent the land from being overrun with tigers.

READING/WRITING CONNECTIONS

1. Tell children that the book you are about to read belongs to a category called *folklore*. These are stories that people tell each other to help them understand nature, other people, and why things are the way they are. Suggest *Little Red Riding Hood* as an example of folklore. Usually these stories are told for generations before someone writes them down.
2. As you show the cover, tell students this book fits International Children's Book Day because Blia Xiong, the author, heard this story as a small child while living in the mountains of Laos.
3. Suggest that students notice the illustrations. They are uniquely Laotian, because they are modeled after the appliqued story cloths of the Laotian people. Lead students in singing Tiger's song.
4. After the story and discussion, divide the students into groups to compose a group story (perhaps a sequel, such as Bird outsmarting another animal). Brainstorm some possibilities. Groups work together writing their stories.
5. Each group designs, on paper, a story cloth that encapsulates or conveys an event in its story.
6. Distribute a large piece of heavy material or material glued to cardboard to each group and have accessible ribbon, beads, twine, other accessories, and smaller pieces of material of various sizes, colors, and textures. Students then construct their story cloths. Glue each written story on the back of its story cloth.

—EXTENSIONS—

LIBRARY CONNECTIONS

1. Engage students in dramatic play. Group 1 enacts Tiger talking to Shao. Group 2 enacts Tiger singing. Group 3 enacts Bird talking to Shao. Group 4 enacts Bird talking to Tiger.
2. Find the country of Laos on a map or globe. Discuss the impact of its location regarding climate, culture, environment, and so forth.

INTEGRATED ACTIVITY

Students calculate how many cubs Tiger would have had in two, five, and ten years if she had not forgotten what Shao told her. (Use manipulatives for younger students.) Then calculate how many cubs she will have in two, five, ten years after Bird's trick. Figure the difference. What would the impact be if Bird hadn't tricked her?

PUBLISHING

Read story cloths and display with book under a banner INTERNATIONAL CHILDREN'S BOOK DAY.

Jackdaw 23

PEBBLES

Earth Day
(April 22)

Title: *A River Ran Wild*. Harcourt Brace Jovanovich, 1992.
Author: Lynne Cherry
Jackdaw: A pebble.
Summary: This book traces the environmental history of the Nashua River, from its pristine condition when it was discovered by Native Americans, through its pollution due to the Industrial Revolution, to its contemporary cleanup and revitalization.

READING/WRITING CONNECTIONS

1. Explain that Earth Day began in 1970 to remind people to celebrate the harmony and balance of the earth.
2. Show the cover. Discuss the possible meanings of the title, especially "ran wild." Examine with students the pictures around the border. Read the "Author's Note." Discuss.
3. After reading the story, distribute pebbles. Divide students into groups of four or five and have each group assign a scribe. Within groups, students brainstorm home and school activities in which they might engage to help protect air, oceans, rivers, streams, animals, trees, and other living things, as the group scribe records the ideas. Share lists.
4. Invite students to make a commitment to undertake at least one of the brainstormed activities and to keep a log of that undertaking. Students might choose recycling paper, collecting aluminum cans, or planting trees.

—EXTENSIONS—

LIBRARY CONNECTIONS

1. Examine the parts of this book. Discuss the significance of the endpapers, the dedication page, the additional information on the copyright page, and the acknowledgments, which help document the story.
2. Help students create banners to hang in the library and around the school to remind everyone of Earth Day.

INTEGRATED ACTIVITY

1. As a class, brainstorm areas in the community that need ecological help.
2. Choose one area to study in depth. Research its history. Use information available in the school library, the public library, the newspaper morgue, and from interviewing senior residents.
3. Following Marion as a model, write persuasive letters to appropriate politicians and residents convincing them to restore the area. To keep the letters from sounding like complaints only, students should make suggestions for concrete, workable solutions.

PUBLISHING

Celebrate EARTH DAY by modeling the book with a mural of the area students chose to restore surrounded by a border of pictures capturing the project. Display students' research to document the story of the restoration.

JACKDAW 23—Copyright 1992 Teacher Ideas Press, a division of Libraries Unlimited, Inc., P.O. Box 6633, Englewood, CO 80155-6633

Jackdaw 24

LEAVES

Arbor Day
(April 22—Often varies, sometimes the last Friday in April)

Title: *A B Cedar: An Alphabet of Trees*. Orchard Books, 1989.

Author: George Ella Lyon

Jackdaw: A leaf.

Summary: This alphabet book shows a silhouette of each tree, its relative size, its shape, and its leaves, fruit, nuts, and flowers, from the aspen to the zebrawood.

READING/WRITING CONNECTIONS

1. Briefly tell the story of J. Sterling Morton, the newspaper editor responsible for Arbor Day. Tell how he, in the interest of conservation, convinced the Nebraska agricultural board to set aside a day to plant trees. Because of his efforts, Arbor Day is a legal holiday.
2. Distribute leaves from different trees, preferably some of those pictured in the book. Ask each student to identify the tree that is the source of his or her leaf. Continue that line of questioning to help students see that leaves can be categorized by characteristics. Speculate on and list what those characteristics might be.
3. Students use the book to find (or check) the names of the trees that bore their leaves. They research some interesting fact about their tree: its origin, its uses, myths associated with it. Share.

—EXTENSIONS—

LIBRARY CONNECTIONS

1. It takes 63,000 trees to create one issue of the Sunday *New York Times*. Have students research other major consumers of trees; what it costs in money, time, and efforts to replenish the supply; and so forth. Choose an area in the community where trees might be planted for beautification or to prevent erosion. Students compile a recommended list of trees the community might choose for that area and provide reasons for their choices. Include information from your research in persuasive letters to the city leaders.
2. Write for a free copy of "Arbor Day News," available from the National Arbor Day Foundation, 100 Arbor Avenue, Nebraska City, NE 68410.

INTEGRATED ACTIVITY

1. Make an enormous drawing of the cross-section of a tree trunk on large brown grocery bags that have been taped together; show growth rings.
2. Working as a large group, students decide after some scientific research the approximate age of the tree. (They must come to a consensus.) Then they label the rings by years.
3. Divide students into small groups. Assign each group a ring and its year. Students must research what was happening in the world during the year that ring was forming on the tree. Write out on index cards.
4. Each group creates an interesting presentation of its findings for the class.

PUBLISHING

Affix the index cards containing researched facts around the cross-section of the tree trunk. Extend string from the card to the appropriate year-ring.

JACKDAW 24—Copyright 1992 Teacher Ideas Press, a division of Libraries Unlimited, Inc., P.O. Box 6633, Englewood, CO 80155-6633

Jackdaw 25

MEMORY BOOKS

MAY
Senior Citizens' Month

Title: *Wilfrid Gordon McDonald Partridge*. Kane/Miller, 1985.
Author: Mem Fox
Jackdaw: A memory book.
Summary: Wilfrid discovers the meaning of memory as he helps Miss Nancy find hers.

READING/WRITING CONNECTIONS

1. Discuss senior citizens, the elderly, and older people the students may know.
2. Before reading the book, speculate on the joys and problems of being a senior citizen.
3. Distribute paper. Students fold into an eight-page book.
   Fold a large piece of paper in half, short end to short end, and crease.
   Fold one side back halfway and crease; fold the other side back halfway and crease.
   Keeping the paper folded, fold it short end to short end and crease.
   Unfold the last fold and allow sides to flip down (looks like a tent).
   Rip or cut carefully down from the peak of the tent, where the center folds meet. Rip or cut only to the next fold.
   Pick the paper up with one hand on either side of the cut. Fold down so the cut is across the top. Recrease the one fold.
   Fold into the shape of a book.
4. After writing the title on the front cover and writing "About the Author" on the back cover, students label the pages: Warm Memories, Memories from Long Ago, Sad Memories, Funny Memories, Precious Memories, and Recent Memories. Students write one memory on each of the appropriate pages. Share. (Students may add to their books throughout the month.)

—EXTENSIONS—

LIBRARY CONNECTIONS

1. Invite several senior citizens to talk to the students or to read or tell a story. Ask guest speakers to share their memories of libraries and their importance.
2. Prepare a basket of memories. Help students do what Wilfrid did, that is, make their memories concrete by finding things to represent them. Add to the basket daily. Invite one student each day to tell about his or her memory. Display the memory basket by the checkout desk for students to enjoy while checking out books.

INTEGRATED ACTIVITY

Interview a senior citizen, about warm, sad, funny, precious, old, and recent memories. Write these up in a memory book and give it to the interviewee after sharing it with the class.

PUBLISHING

Display memory books on a bulletin board entitled GOLDEN YEARS.

JACKDAW 25—Copyright 1992 Teacher Ideas Press, a division of Libraries Unlimited, Inc., P.O. Box 6633, Englewood, CO 80155-6633

Jackdaw 26

MAY FLOWERS

May Day
(May 1)

Title: *Happy Holidaysaurus!* Harcourt Brace Jovanovich, 1992.
Author: Bernard Most
Jackdaw: A May flower.
Summary: This book presents holidays with a "saurus" twist. For example, Happy Maysaurus Day! connects the customs of May Day to the characteristics of the brachiosaurus.

READING/WRITING CONNECTIONS
1. Tell students that today is May Day. This holiday comes to us from England, where people celebrated the season by watching dancers circle around a Maypole and giving baskets of fruits and flowers to each other.
2. Show and read the page that pictures brachiosaurus's neck acting as a Maypole.
3. Arrange the students in a circle around some tall, familiar object in the room. Let them skip around as if it were a Maypole. Then have them skip to "Here we go round the Maypole," sung as an adaptation of "Here we go round the mulberry bush." (Just add an extra syllable to make the word *Maypole* fit in place of the words *mulberry bush*.
4. Tell students the next time they skip around the Maypole, they will carry flowers to toss, just as is done on May Day in England.
5. Distribute colored tissues and pipe cleaners. Students bunch the tissue in the middle and secure it with the pipe cleaner to make a "flower." Give each student a basket to fill with flowers for this activity (borrow some if necessary).
6. Skip around the Maypole again, singing the Maypole/mulberry bush variation. This time the students will have to concentrate on doing three things: skipping, singing, and tossing their flowers.

—EXTENSIONS—

LIBRARY CONNECTIONS
1. Read the other pages in the book. Talk about holidays and find them on a calendar.
2. Advanced students make up other holidaysaurus pages. Brainstorm holidays not mentioned in the book. Brainstorm different dinosaurs. Let the students play with both lists until they come up with an idea for a page. Students write their holidaysaurus page. Share.

INTEGRATED ACTIVITY
Look at the month of May on the calendar. Count the number of days in May. Talk about what month came before May and what month comes after May. Talk about things that happen in May.

PUBLISHING
Make large letters which read HAPPY HOLIDAYSAURUS! for the bulletin board. Display students' work.

JACKDAW 26—Copyright 1992 Teacher Ideas Press, a division of Libraries Unlimited, Inc., P.O. Box 6633, Englewood, CO 80155-6633

Jackdaw 27

CORN CHIPS

Cinco de Mayo
(May 5)

Title: *Fiesta! Cinco de Mayo*. Childrens Press, 1978. (Book is available in both Spanish and English.)

Author: June Behrens

Jackdaw: Small bags of corn chips.

Summary: This book describes, through words and photographs, what happens during the colorful and exciting celebration of Cinco de Mayo.

READING/WRITING CONNECTIONS

1. Distribute the small bags of corn chips, play some Mexican music, and introduce this holiday to the students. Explain that on this day Mexicans and Mexican-Americans commemorate the defeat of Napoleon III's powerful French army by a ragged and poor but determined army, led by General Ignacio Zarogoza, at the Battle of Pueblo in 1862. It is considered *la gloriosa fecha* (glorious date) because the Mexican army overcame great odds and kept the French from accomplishing Napoleon's dream of a permanent settlement in Central America.

2. After the reading, distribute paper in neon colors. Students write about some festival or holiday they celebrate in their culture. Share.

—EXTENSIONS—

LIBRARY CONNECTIONS

1. Involve students in a Cinco de Mayo project for the library. Distribute several pieces of brightly colored tissue paper to each student. Explain that they will make a variation of *papel picado* (pierced paper). Cut the tissue into 10" x 18" pieces. Fold the pieces smaller. Cut out designs. Open the tissue to see exciting patterns. Roll one end of the papel picado to form a border roll; insert string through this border and tape. Suspend from string and hang around the library.

2. Have some "Fun with Words" from Westridge Young Writers Workshop's book *Kids Explore America's Hispanic Heritage*. This chapter offers *dichos* (sayings), *chistes* (jokes), *adivinanzas* (riddles), *los colores* (colors), *frases* (phrases), cognates, and Spanish place-names. Or celebrate by reading one of the *cuentos* (stories) such as "El Grillo" (The Cricket).

INTEGRATED ACTIVITY

1. Divide the class into groups. Each group makes a shopping bag piñata. Provide the shopping bags, and crepe paper, yarn, glue, tape, glitter, stickers, stars, etc.

2. As students finish their piñatas, but before they tie them, put some treats in the bags.

3. Individual members of each group, blindfolded and armed with rolled magazines or newspapers, attempt to be the one to break the piñata.

PUBLISHING

Extend an invitation to parents to attend the class's Cinco de Mayo fiesta!

JACKDAW 27—Copyright 1992 Teacher Ideas Press, a division of Libraries Unlimited, Inc., P.O. Box 6633, Englewood, CO 80155-6633

Jackdaw 28

ANIMAL CRACKERS

Be Kind to Animals Week
(May: The first week)

Title: *I'll Always Love You*. Crown, 1985.

Author: Hans Wilhelm

Jackdaw: Animal crackers.

Summary: The narrator is a young boy who grows up with his dog Elfie. When Elfie dies, the young boy takes comfort in the fact that every night he told Elfie, "I'll always love you."

READING/WRITING CONNECTIONS

1. Tell students this is Be Kind to Animals Week. Speculate about the purpose of such a week.
2. Explain that you have a special book to share for this week. Students describe what is happening on the cover. Ask students what pets need from us. Ask students what pets give to us.
3. After the reading, ask students how they feel about Elfie and how they feel about the young boy. Talk about what thoughts made the boy feel less sad after the family buried Elfie.
4. Speculate about why the boy did not take the puppy the neighbor offered.
5. Ask students what they think about when they hear the word *pet*. Write their responses on the board or chart. Encourage students to talk about pets they have had or wish to have. Distribute animal crackers. Students write how they would take care of the animal in the animal cracker if they had it for a pet. Share.

—EXTENSIONS—

LIBRARY CONNECTIONS

Choose several nonfiction books about domesticated animals. Show students the pictures. Students identify the animals, imitate the sounds they make, and imitate the way they move. Students engage in dramatic play on the care and feeding of animals. Contrast with how to care for and feed wild animals.

INTEGRATED ACTIVITY

Students measure and make the following recipe for their pets:

Rye Crisps

2 cups rye flour 6 tablespoons oil
¼ cup white flour ⅔ cup warm water
¼ cup cornmeal

Directions: Preheat oven to 350°F. Mix flours and cornmeal. Mix oil with water. Add to flour. Mix well. Roll dough into a ball. Pat dough out (about ¼" thickness) onto a oiled cookie sheet. Bake until brown. Cool. Break into medium-sized pieces. Serve with love to a pet.

PUBLISHING

Make a pet house out of a box. With students, write on large pieces of cardboard the things they should remember about taking care of pets and being kind to animals. Students place these cards in and around the pet house.

Jackdaw 29

POP-UP CARDS

Mother's Day
(May: Second Sunday)

Title: *Mama, Do You Love Me?* Chronicle Books, 1991.
Author: Barbara M. Joosse
Jackdaw: A pop-up card.
Summary: By asking questions, an Inuit child learns that her mother's love is unconditional.

READING/WRITING CONNECTIONS

1. Use masks, carved boxes, carvings, or figurines done by the Inuit, prints by Barbara Lavallee (the illustrator of this book), or pictures of Inuit art to establish the setting for the book.
2. If students respond to prediction questions about the book by calling the characters "Eskimos," read the statement in the back of the book about the Inuit.
3. Before reading the book, read the two pages in the back that highlight certain aspects of Inuit culture. Explain that even though it is important to understand the cultural background of this book, this mother/daughter event could take place anywhere, in any country. Introduce or review the concept of universality, as applied to universal themes in literature.
4. Divide students into groups to brainstorm a series of questions they might ask their mothers or care givers and answers they might receive. Use the book as a model. Students then create a Mother's Day pop-up card using the question-and-answer format. (See Integrated Activity.)

—EXTENSIONS—

LIBRARY CONNECTIONS

1. After telling students that Mother's Day began in 1908, because of the initiative of Anna Jarvis, invite them to use the resources in the library to find an appropriate quotation to write on a bookmark (a strip of light-weight cardboard) for their mothers.
2. Laminate bookmarks or cover with contact paper. Students cut away the extra laminate, punch a hole in the bottom of the bookmark, and tie a ribbon through the hole.

INTEGRATED ACTIVITY

Make Mother's Day pop-up cards. Distribute a standard 12" file folder to each student. Students: 1. Cut off any tabs. On the fold, measuring in from one side, mark at 3", 6", 8", and 10". 2. Measure and draw a 3" square using the fold as one side and the 3" and 6" marks as two other sides. Join the pencil rules at the top, parallel to the fold, to complete the square. Do the same, using the marks at 8" and 10" to make a 2" square. 3. Cut along the vertical lines of each square (from the fold toward the top of the folder). 4. Push the squares through to the inside of the folder, inverting the crease, to form the pop-outs. Use the pencil marks as guides to crease the edges of each pop-out. (When the pop-outs are folded in, the back of the card will look like a block letter E.) 5. Cover the card with pastel-colored paper so that the cut-out sections do not show. 6. Paste or draw pictures on the pop-outs. 7. Write the series of questions and answers from the Reading/Writing Connection inside the card. 8. Decorate the outside of the card.

PUBLISHING

Share cards in a Mother's Day Read-Around.

JACKDAW 29—Copyright 1992 Teacher Ideas Press, a division of Libraries Unlimited, Inc., P.O. Box 6633, Englewood, CO 80155-6633

Jackdaw 30

PENCIL RUBBINGS

Memorial Day
(May 30—Often observed the last Monday in May)

Title: *The Wall.* Clarion Books, 1990.

Author: Eve Bunting

Jackdaw: A pencil rubbing.

Summary: A father and son visit the Vietnam Veterans Memorial in Washington, D.C. There they find the name of the boy's grandfather, who was killed in the conflict.

READING/WRITING CONNECTIONS

1. Write the word *memorial* on the board. Create a word web of associations. Then explain that Memorial Day, once called Decoration Day, began when people decorated the graves of those who died in the Civil War. Today Americans remember and honor the dead of all wars.
2. Show the front cover of the book. Discuss. Show the back cover. Discuss.
3. After reading the book, let students do pencil rubbings like the one in the book. They place two pieces of paper on top of one another. Pressing heavily on the top sheet, they print their names. After removing the top sheet, an impression will be seen in the second page. Then they put a sheet of tracing paper, thin typing paper, or Oriental paper over the impression and rub over it with the side of a soft pencil.
4. Under the pencil rubbings, students write to the family or friend of a person who died while serving in the armed forces. Share.

—EXTENSIONS—

LIBRARY CONNECTIONS

1. Display books involving U.S. armed conflicts. Discuss. Locate, in an atlas or on a map or globe, the sites of wars in which the United States was involved.
2. If possible, make available *The Wall: Images and Offerings from the Vietnam Veterans Memorial*, conceived by Sal Lopes. This book captures feelings and images about the Vietnam Veterans Memorial (often called The Wall) through photography and extends Bunting's book.

INTEGRATED ACTIVITY

1. Provide students with data about the wall. In groups, students create either a mathematical word problem entailing computations, or a social studies problem requiring research.

    58,132 names listed chronologically according to death date appear on two walls. Each wall is 246.75 feet long. They meet at an angle of 125 degrees. The walls are 10.1 feet high. Each wall has 70 panels. The wall was conceived by Jan C. Scruggs. The wall was designed by Maya Ying Lin.

2. Exchange with other groups. Groups work out answers.

PUBLISHING

Create a black bulletin board titled THE WALL. Display rubbings and writing done by students. Add books, pictures, letters, flags, and anything else related to Memorial Day.

Jackdaw 31

FLAGS

JUNE, JULY, AUGUST
Flag Day
(June 14)

Title: *The Star-Spangled Banner*. Doubleday, 1973.

Author: Peter Spier

Jackdaw: A small American flag.

Summary: This book contains beautifully illustrated pages to accompany the words of the national anthem, historical information about how it came to be written, a reproduction of Francis Scott Key's original manuscript, and the music for those who would like to sing or play "The Star-Spangled Banner." Perhaps most interesting are the pages showing a collection of American flags.

READING/WRITING CONNECTIONS

1. Show students the double-page spread of flags at the opening of the book. Ask who can find the first official American flag (the Stars and Stripes, June 14, 1777). Discuss some of the other flags pictured.
2. Ask students to think of times flags were used throughout history. Speculate on why flags were used. Help students picture the era, topography, and ancient battles. Ask students if they can think of ways flags are used as signals (half-mast, a white flag, or an inverted flag). Discuss.
3. Discuss symbols. Talk about flags as symbols.
4. Distribute small pieces of paper and ask students to write the number of stars and number of stripes on the present American flag. Distribute small flags and let students check their answers. Discuss the significance of those numbers. Examine the growth of the United States through the changes in the flags pictured.
5. Read the book. Stop often to discuss the illustrations.

—EXTENSIONS—

LIBRARY CONNECTIONS

Provide students with access to areas in the library where they may find more information on Francis Scott Key, the Battle of Baltimore, historical societies, the Star-Spangled Banner Flag House in Baltimore, Mary Young Pickergill, and the Smithsonian Institution.

INTEGRATED ACTIVITY

1. Flag Day is not a legal holiday. Divide students into groups to generate two lists. One list contains reasons supporting the argument that Flag Day should be designated a legal holiday. The other list contains reasons supporting its present status. Share and discuss lists.
2. Students may use these lists as prewriting for a persuasive paper.

PUBLISHING

Display students writing on a red, white, and blue 'TIS THE STAR-SPANGLED BANNER bulletin board.

JACKDAW 31—Copyright 1992 Teacher Ideas Press, a division of Libraries Unlimited, Inc., P.O. Box 6633, Englewood, CO 80155-6633

Jackdaw 32

SAILBOATS

Father's Day
(June: Third Sunday)

Title: *My Father*. Little, Brown & Co., 1968.
Author: Judy Collins
Jackdaw: An origami sailboat.
Summary: Judy Collins wrote the lyrics and music (provided at the beginning of the book) about a father's dreams of the finer things in life: music, dance, travel. Those dreams sustained the family during their drab life in an Ohio mining town and were ultimately fulfilled by his daughter.

READING/WRITING CONNECTIONS

1. Tell students that we honor fathers this week. Talk about fathers, their responsibilities, and their role in the family. Older students may talk about the changing roles of fathers.
2. Play the music (and sing the words) to *My Father*. Read the book and discuss.
3. Write the line, "On his streams like boats we knew we'd sail in time." Students think about what that line might mean, and then write their ideas on a slip of paper. Share.
4. Talk about the symbolism of boats. Students make origami sailboats. Use papers and instructions from Yasutomo & Co., Brisbane, CA 94005 (available in most craft stores) or in any good origami instruction book. They write their goals on the side of the boats. Display and discuss.

—EXTENSIONS—

LIBRARY CONNECTIONS

On globes, atlases, and maps, students locate the places stated in the book: France, the Seine, Denver, Cheyenne, Paris, and Ohio. Have them calculate the travel time to each place. They write one interesting fact about each place. Share.

INTEGRATED ACTIVITY

1. Students interview their fathers (or care givers) about where they would like to travel if they had the means. They use the Reporter's Formula: What? Where? Why? When? Who? How?
2. Students create an itinerary for their fathers or care givers: They: a. Map out the route, including the type of travel and all alternate means of travel. b. Provide a detailed plan for the journey, with a list of places to visit, hotels, restaurants, and suggested sights to see. c. Figure the time involved. d. Calculate the cost.
3. Each student packages his or her itinerary in some uniquely appropriate way, complete with such things as pictures, travel brochures (available at travel agencies), music, a clothing catalogue, and guides.

PUBLISHING

Before taking them home as Father's Day gifts, students share their itineraries in small groups.

Jackdaw 33   BUTTERFLIES

Summer Solstice
(June 21 or 22)

Title: *I Wish I Were a Butterfly*. Harcourt Brace Jovanovich, 1987.

Author: James Howe

Jackdaw: A miniature butterfly (available in craft stores).

Summary: A cricket with low self-esteem is helped by a wise spider.

READING/WRITING CONNECTIONS

1. Introduce the book by asking students to think about summer. Explain that today is the summer solstice. Today the earth is tilted so that the North Pole is its closest to the sun, so the summer solstice is the longest day of the year and the shortest night. Tell them you have a special book to share to help celebrate this season.

2. Hold the book open so students get the full effect of the butterfly on the dust jacket. Write the word *butterfly* on the board and ask students to brainstorm words that describe it. When someone offers *beautiful*, use that adjective to encourage deeper thinking about the nature of beauty and what makes something beautiful.

3. Distribute a miniature butterfly to each student and ask each student to write a sequel to Howe's story. They are to begin with, "What beautiful music that creature makes. I wish I were a cricket." They may want to continue with the theme of beauty, or they may want to write about summer, but a butterfly should be in the story. Share.

—EXTENSIONS—

LIBRARY CONNECTIONS

1. Share two books with students to extend Howe's book: Eric Carle's *The Very Quiet Cricket* and Maria M. Mudd's *The Butterfly*. Complete a Venn diagram on these insects' characteristics. Discuss.

2. Take students on a nature hunt. Divide students into teams. They list as many beautiful things as they can find during this walk. Caution students that they should be prepared to defend their choices. After the walk, share lists and discuss the choices.

INTEGRATED ACTIVITY

1. Students may research some of the butterflies of the tropical rain forest: Scamander, *Anteos menippe*, Passion-flower, *Siproeta stelenes*, *Papilio androgeus*, *Hamadryas arinome*, Blue morpho, *Vindula arsinoe*, and Urania.

2. To share their research, students anthropomorphise their butterflies by attributing human characteristics to them. That way the subject of their research can talk, think, and feel.

PUBLISHING

Construct a huge butterfly (wire works well). Suspend it from the ceiling in the middle of the room with students' work hanging from it for a SUMMER FLUTTERS BY display.

JACKDAW 33—Copyright 1992 Teacher Ideas Press, a division of Libraries Unlimited, Inc., P.O. Box 6633, Englewood, CO 80155-6633

Jackdaw 34

PINWHEELS

Independence Day
(July 4)

Title: *Doodle Dandy! The Complete Book of Independence Day Words*. Bradbury Press, 1992.

Author: Lynda Graham-Barber

Jackdaw: A pinwheel.

Summary: A nonfiction book that defines, explains, and gives the etymology and historical background of words usually associated with Independence Day.

READING/WRITING CONNECTIONS

1. Distribute thick red, white, or blue pencils with erasers, 4" square red or blue origami paper, and straight pins. Students fold the paper diagonally to get crisscross creases. Cut on creases to within ¼" of the center point. Stick a pin through alternating points of the paper and into the pencil's eraser. Remind students that waving flags, streamers, and pinwheels are ways people celebrate at Fourth of July parades.

2. Explain that it was on July 4, 1776, that the Continental Congress approved the Declaration of Independence. Read all or portions of the Declaration from pages 54-65. Discuss.

3. Read "Independence Day" (pages 2-6) and the "Do You Know" (page 7). Discuss.

4. Write all the words referenced in the book on slips of paper. Each student draws one word and writes everything he or she can think of associated with that word, especially how it might be associated with July 4. Invite several volunteers to read their lists.

5. Challenge students to further research their word, to read about it in this book, to present their word in a creative way to the class, and to make it part of the Fourth of July decor of the classroom or library.

—EXTENSIONS—

LIBRARY CONNECTIONS

Spread pieces of butcher paper on the floor for a reading-and-writing picnic. Read page 99. Invite students to tell about their experiences with picnics. Then each "picnic group" writes its version of the ideal picnic. Share.

INTEGRATED ACTIVITY

1. Give students a copy of the Declaration of Independence, run off on light blue paper.

2. Tell students to think of this document as a persuasive essay. Students color code their analyses by underlining or highlighting the statement (proposition) plus any restatements in red, arguments (points) in blue, and support for those arguments in yellow. Divide into groups to share and discuss the analyses.

3. Students create a meaningful border, using any of Jan Brett's books, to illustrate the Declaration.

PUBLISHING

To celebrate Independence Day, decorate the room and the bulletin board in red, white, and blue. Create time-line banners. Display words students have researched. Exhibit color-coded Declarations. Create colorful fireworks on paper. Sing patriotic songs and play recordings of John Philip Sousa marches, especially "Semper Fidelis" and "The Stars and Stripes Forever."

Jackdaw 35

CHERRY BLOSSOMS

Peace Day
(August 6)

Title: *My Hiroshima*. Viking, 1987.
Author: Junko Morimoto
Title: *The Cherry Tree*. Alfred A. Knopf, 1991.
Author: Daisaku Ikeda
Jackdaw: Popcorn cherry blossoms.
Summary: The first book tells of Morimoto's childhood in Hiroshima before and after the dropping of the atomic bomb. The second book beautifully conveys that even after the bomb's devastation, the Japanese people never gave up hope.

READING/WRITING CONNECTIONS

1. Discuss the pictures on both books' dust jackets. Explain that the atomic bomb was dropped on Hiroshima on August 6, 1945. Speculate on the devastation following the dropping of the bomb.
2. Celebrate the hope reflected in *The Cherry Tree* by making popcorn cherry blossoms: a. On white cardboard, draw some tree branches with brown markers and leaves with green markers. b. Put a handful or two of popped corn in a plastic bag. Add several drops of red food coloring (or red and white tempera paint) and shake the bag. c. Glue the colored popcorn on the branches to simulate cherry blossoms.
3. Students write a Peace Day commemoration on their cherry blossom branches. Share.

—EXTENSIONS—

LIBRARY CONNECTIONS

Before the bomb, Morimoto played games like "Oranges and Lemons." After the bomb, Taichi and Yumiko played games on rubble heaps. Help students locate information on games of children around the world. Identify games that are just like the students' games. Learn to play an unfamiliar game.

INTEGRATED ACTIVITY

1. After reading "The Facts about Hiroshima" in *My Hiroshima*, perform an experiment with light waves so students may better understand the principles of radiation: a. Fold black construction paper over an outdoor thermometer; staple sides. b. Fold aluminum foil over a second outdoor thermometer; secure sides by folding over. c. Record temperature on both thermometers. d. Place a 100-watt light bulb about one foot above the thermometers. e. Turn light on for 10 minutes. f. Take another reading from both thermometers.
2. Students write up results, draw conclusions, and connect to nuclear radiation. (Adapted from Janice VanCleave's *Chemistry for Every Kid*.)

PUBLISHING

Create a large cherry tree along one wall of the classroom out of twisted brown paper bags. Exhibit Peace Day Commemorations around the tree.

JACKDAW 35—Copyright 1992 Teacher Ideas Press, a division of Libraries Unlimited, Inc., P.O. Box 6633, Englewood, CO 80155-6633

Jackdaw 36

STEEL WOOL PADS

SEPTEMBER
Labor Day
(September: First Monday)

Title: *No Star Nights*. Alfred A. Knopf, 1989.

Author: Anna Egan Smucker

Jackdaw: A piece of steel from a steel wool pad.

Summary: A little girl of the 1950s describes the steel-mill town of her childhood, where everyone's father worked in the mill.

READING/WRITING CONNECTIONS

1. Begin by explaining that Labor Day was instituted as a national holiday in 1894 to honor people who work by giving them a holiday, a day off work.
2. Distribute small pieces of steel from steel wool pads. Invite students to describe how it feels, smells, looks, and sounds when it is rubbed. Talk about the source of steel and the steel-making process iron must go through to remove its impurities. Invite students to speculate on what it must be like to work in those steel mills.
3. With that introduction, read the book.
4. After the reading, students write how they feel about the book and about Labor Day. Share and discuss.

—EXTENSIONS—

LIBRARY CONNECTIONS

1. Reread the book. This time invite students to jot down all the words they hear that evoke sensory images—words and phrases such as *spark-spitting, fiery hot, loud bang, smell of lemons, being stung, drinking lemonade, looked like a dinosaur*.
2. Divide the class into groups. Each group receives a large piece of butcher paper, which they divide into five columns. They label one column Sight, another Touch, the third Taste, the fourth Hearing, and the last Smell. Using words from the pool previously generated, assign each word or phrase to a column.
3. Using reference books, groups locate synonyms and antonyms for the words in their columns.
4. Share results. Discuss the power of using sensory imagery in writing.

INTEGRATED WRITING

Divide students into teams of "economists" (adapt for grade level). Each team writes an economic history of the West Virginia mill town in the book. Each team: 1) gives the town a name; 2) provides its population; 3) tells how many work at the steel mill; 4) gives the average salary; 5) states the workers' vacation pay; 6) estimates the year the steel mill shut down; 7) suggests reasons for its closing; 8) describes the economy of the town in the present year; 9) makes a forecast.

PUBLISHING

Share the economic histories. Display on a bulletin board labelled WE LABORED ON LABOR DAY! Conclude by singing the song mentioned in the book, "She'll Be Comin' Round the Mountain."

Jackdaw 37

FISH PRINTS

Grandparents' Day
(September: First Sunday after Labor Day)

Title: *The Great Change*. Beyond Words, 1992.

Author: Gabriel Horn (White Deer of Autumn)

Jackdaw: A fish print.

Summary: An American Indian grandmother explains the meaning of death to her granddaughter, who questions death in nature and the death of her grandfather.

READING/WRITING CONNECTIONS

1. Hold a grab bag and allow each student to pull out some everyday object (string, cork, a piece of aluminum, a book, and so forth). Ask students to place their objects on their desks and to write an exact description of the way the object looks.
2. Tell the students to change the object in some way and then write about that change.
3. Use that object lesson to introduce the concept of change. Share Grandma's words, "Nothing stays the same, my girl, all things change." Discuss. Ask what a book titled *The Great Change* might be about. Read and discuss the book.
4. Ask students how Grandma and Wanba changed the fish they caught. Discuss the symbolism of fish. Tell students that they too will change fish. Give each small group a frozen, partly frozen, or chilled fish. (Lay the fish on plenty of newspaper or paper towels.) Students paint the surface of the fish with colored inks or tempera paint. Quickly but gently they lay lightweight paper over the fish and press to imprint the fish.
5. Students write a poem or story about change, grandparents, love, or some other related theme. Laminate fish prints and writing for display or for gifts for grandparents.

—EXTENSIONS—

LIBRARY CONNECTIONS

1. Tell students that Marian McQuade initiated Grandparents' Day as a way of thanking grandparents. Help students find more information on McQuade by using library resources.
2. Share and display other books about grandparents. See Carroll's *Story Books*, Jackdaw 24. Invite students to choose one to read to a partner. Discuss grandparents. Have students check out a favorite to share with a grandparent or older family friend.

INTEGRATED ACTIVITY

1. The caterpillar and cocoon became the major sign Grandma needed to help Wanba understand death as change. Write to Carolina Biological Supply Company or other dealers of biological supplies (see bibliography) for cocoon (chrysalis or pupa) specimens.
2. Students keep a notebook of their research and observations of the cocoons' metamorphoses.

PUBLISHING

HONOR GRANDPARENTS DAY! Invite grandparents to visit. Present them with the laminated fish prints and writing. Some grandparents may wish to share some of their stories (or writing) with students.

JACKDAW 37—Copyright 1992 Teacher Ideas Press, a division of Libraries Unlimited, Inc., P.O. Box 6633, Englewood, CO 80155-6633

Jackdaw 38

TRI-FOLDS

Autumnal Equinox
(September 22 or 23)

Title: "Autumnal Equinox" in Janeczko's *The Music of What Happens: Poems That Tell Stories*. Orchard Books, 1988.

Author: Edward E. Wilson

Jackdaw: A tri-folded response paper.

Summary: The narrator tells how an experience at harvest time jolted him from his childhood into adulthood.

READING/WRITING CONNECTIONS

1. Inform students that today is the autumnal equinox, when day and night will be of equal length all over the world. Before reading the poem, remind students to listen carefully so they can participate in a tri-fold response following the reading.
2. Read the poem. Without discussion, students fold a plain sheet of paper in thirds.
3. In the middle third, students write what struck them most in the poem, for example: an unusual word, an image, a phrase, something they remember from the poem.
4. In the top third, students write whatever happened before what they wrote in the middle section. (If students wrote the first line or the title, they infer what came before.)
5. In the lower third, students write whatever happened after what they wrote in the middle section. (If students wrote the last line or word, they predict what happens next.)
6. Divide students into small groups. Each student shares his or her paper by reading the middle section first, then the other two sections. Discuss what is alike and different in the responses. As a class, discuss what caused those like and different responses.

—EXTENSIONS—

LIBRARY CONNECTIONS

1. Divide students into groups. Ask groups to arrive at a consensus on two things: the approximate year the story in the poem takes place and the geographical location of the poem. Students may check or research any details in the poem as they discuss possibilities.
2. Help students use library resources to check on other things from the poem that might help the group reach a consensus, such as the authenticity of a Swisher County, when "Dear Abby" appeared in the newspapers, and so forth.
3. Groups share their decisions, explaining their reasons. Discuss.

INTEGRATED ACTIVITY

Divide the class in half. One half writes persuasively in favor of the poem's title; the other half writes persuasively that the title does not work.

PUBLISHING

Share persuasive pieces, then tack the pros on one side of a corn shock that has been affixed to the center of a bulletin board and the cons on the other. Title the display AUTUMNAL EQUINOX.

JACKDAW 38—Copyright 1992 Teacher Ideas Press, a division of Libraries Unlimited, Inc., P.O. Box 6633, Englewood, CO 80155-6633

Jackdaw 39 — BONES

National Dog Week
(September: Begins the Sunday of the last full week)

Title: *The First Dog*. Harcourt Brace Jovanovich, 1988.

Author: Jan Brett

Jackdaw: A rhino bone.

Summary: A cave boy named Kip meets up with a Paleowolf in dangerous Paleolithic times. They join forces and Paleowolf becomes the first dog.

READING/WRITING CONNECTIONS

1. Explain to students that this is National Dog Week. Students talk about the dogs they have had in their lives, either as pets, friends' pets, or dogs they have seen in neighborhoods. Conclude by wondering about how the first dog came to be.
2. Before showing the book's jacket, title, or author, open to the endpapers. Invite students to identify the animals shown. Ask them to speculate on the time period. Then introduce the book.
3. Read the "Publisher's Note" and examine the borders. Discuss what Kip is doing and who is watching. Talk about reasons why Paleowolf does not attack Kip.
4. After the reading, students write a sequel to the adventures of Kip and Dog.
5. Make an enormous papier-mâché bone out of paper tubes and newspaper. Crush a newspaper ball and fit into one end of the tube. With masking tape, secure the newspaper ball. Wrap the bones with strips of newspaper (dipped into a gluey mixture of flour and water the consistency of gravy) to achieve the desired shape. Dry and paint with white tempera. Tape stories to the bone and display.

—EXTENSIONS—

LIBRARY CONNECTIONS

1. Share other dog books: Pauline Bayne's *How Dog Began* gives another version on how the first dog was tamed; Ruth Brown's *Our Puppy's Vacation* takes readers on a vacation with a lovable Labrador puppy; Abigail Pizer's *Nosey Gilbert* shows what can happen to misplaced, mischievous curiosity; Marjorie Weinman Sharmat's *I'm the Best!* tells the story of a "foster" dog who finds a home; Susan Breslow's *I Really Want a Dog* conveys a child's longing for a dog; Norman Bridwell's *Clifford the Big Red Dog* chronicles Emily Elizabeth's adventures with her unusual dog; Alexandra Day's *Carl's Christmas* shows exactly, without words, how Carl the dog takes care of the baby on Christmas Eve.
2. Have students research famous, heroic, and literary dogs. Make a chart that classifies the dogs.

INTEGRATED ACTIVITY

Decorate the room with Spanish moss and introduce the Pleistocene geologic era (referred to in the book) as roughly coextensive with the Stone Age. Students read and research this period, after which they construct shoe-box dioramas of period scenes, complete with written text to accompany them.

PUBLISHING

Display students' dioramas and text, bones and stories under a banner PLEISTOCENE GEOLOGIC ERA.

Jackdaw 40

APPLE SLICES AND HONEY

SEPTEMBER/OCTOBER
Rosh Hashanah
(First day of the Hebrew month Tishri)

Title: *A Jewish Holiday A B C*. Harcourt Brace Jovanovich, 1992.

Authors: Malka Drucker and Rita Pocock

Jackdaw: An apple slice and tiny cups of honey.

Summary: An alphabet book that introduces the Jewish holidays from the *afikomen* of the Seder to the singing of *Shabbat zemirot*.

READING/WRITING CONNECTIONS

1. Explain that Rosh Hashanah marks the Jewish New Year. Distribute apple slices and cups of honey. As students eat, discuss the custom of dipping apples in honey to bring sweetness to them during the New Year. Ask students to describe what their apples taste like.
2. Read the book, stopping to talk especially about Rosh Hashanah.
3. Blow a small horn. Explain to students that during Rosh Hashanah a ram's horn is blown to "awaken" Jews to think about how they behaved during the year that is ending. Invite students to sit quietly and think about how they behaved during the past several days. Encourage students to share their thoughts.
4. Groups generate a list of words associated with Rosh Hashanah. Then they write individual stories about how they celebrate the holiday. Share.

—EXTENSIONS—

LIBRARY CONNECTIONS

1. Look at the parts of this book with students. Talk about the colors of the endpapers, discuss the significance of the picture opposite the title page, read the section "About the Holidays," and point out the glossary.
2. Have students research the role of foods for other religious groups. Discuss the importance of food in all sorts of activities and observations: birthdays, holidays, popcorn at the movies, and so forth.

INTEGRATED ACTIVITY

1. Students study the shapes that are associated with the holiday: a. Circle for apples. b. Spiral shape of the ram's horn and the holiday loaves. c. Rectangle for the sheets in the Torah. d. Triangle for the two triangles that make the Star of David. e. Square for the holiday table.
2. Then each student makes a book called "The Shapes of Rosh Hashanah." Each page will have a different shape, color, and some information written by the students. (Older students may add other shapes and explanations associated with the holiday.)

PUBLISHING

Display books around the room. Sing "Happy Birthday" to celebrate the birth of the New Year. Conclude by wishing each other "Peace" by using the Hebrew word *shalom*.

Jackdaw 41

PIZZA-FLAVORED CRACKERS

OCTOBER
National Pizza Month

Title: *Pizza for Breakfast*. Morrow Junior Books, 1991.

Author: Maryann Kovalski

Jackdaw: Pizza-flavored crackers or chips.

Summary: Frank and Zelda learn that planning, not wishing, yields the best results.

READING/WRITING CONNECTIONS

1. Distribute crackers. Invite students to taste them and conjecture about the flavor.
2. Discuss pizza: kinds, sources, homemade versus store-bought, and pizza-eating occasions.
3. Talk about eating pizza for breakfast. Show the cover and discuss what is happening. Predict what might happen. Show the title page; discuss the illustrations in relation to students' predictions.
4. Attending to the illustrations on the two-page dedication spread, invite speculation on the era, neighborhood, geographical region of the country, and season. Students hold that image in their minds as they compare and contrast it to the cover and to the illustration on the next two-page spread. Then ask if students want to reevaluate their original predictions. Discuss.
5. Read through the story, stopping after, "They sipped their tea and made their plan." Pair students to write a plan and a reason for that plan. Read the last page. Discuss Frank and Zelda's plan; speculate on their reasons for it. Students share their plans and reasons and compare and contrast theirs with Frank and Zelda's.
6. Conclude with a discussion on the purpose and wisdom of making plans.

—EXTENSIONS—

LIBRARY CONNECTIONS

Divide students into "Pizza Research" teams. Encourage the use of library resources, including various consumer reports. Work with the business pages of the telephone book to classify the number and locations of stores so that students contact a variety of stores. Help students prepare a telephone interview with pizza shop and grocery store owners. Teach students to introduce themselves by saying, "I am conducting a pizza survey for a school project. May I ask you a few questions?" Questions might be one such as, "What is your most popular selling pizza?" Teams compare and discuss findings.

INTEGRATED ACTIVITY

1. Brainstorm with students ingredients that might serve as pizza toppings.
2. Students construct a grid with these ingredients and the names of 10 consumers.
3. Acting as market analysts, students conduct surveys by polling the pizza-topping preferences of the consumers on their grids. They enter these on the grid.
4. Based on the information on their grids, students write a report of their conclusions.

PUBLISHING

Celebrate surveys and National Pizza Month with a reading of reports and a PIZZA PARTY!

JACKDAW 41—Copyright 1992 Teacher Ideas Press, a division of Libraries Unlimited, Inc., P.O. Box 6633, Englewood, CO 80155-6633

Jackdaw 42

SEASHELLS

Universal Children's Day
(October 3)

Title: *One World*. Arcade, 1990.

Arthor: Michael Foreman

Jackdaw: A seashell.

Summary: Two children, playing on the beach, realize the interconnectedness of everything and everyone in the universe.

READING/WRITING CONNECTIONS

1. Read the first page and talk about what those first four lines mean. Tell students this is Universal Children's Day, a day celebrating the time in 1954 when the United Nations General Assembly, composed of representatives from all over the world, convened to work toward peace. They believed that if children understood children from other countries, they would work together more easily when they became adults.
2. Tell students to keep that idea in mind as you read. After the reading, discuss the meaning of the book and how it connects to the theme of this day.
3. Divide students into small groups and distribute seashells. The group's task is to study their shells and write a connection between them and Universal Children's Day. They also write how they came up with that connection and why they think it is valid. Share.

—EXTENSIONS—

LIBRARY CONNECTIONS

Collect and display books that reflect the life and culture of people in other countries. Divide the class into pairs. Each pair chooses a book to "buddy read." When they have completed the reading, they should be encouraged to talk about the book and answer these questions:
1. What did you learn about other people through your reading?
2. What did you learn about reading and working with another person?

Share responses and then discuss how those responses might apply to everyone everywhere.

INTEGRATED ACTIVITY

The United Nations International Children's Emergency Fund (UNICEF) assists children and adolescents worldwide, particularly in devastated areas and developing countries. The book says that all children live in one world and that the world is in their hands. Divide the class into action teams. Distribute long sheets of butcher paper. Each team:
1. Chooses one country where UNICEF is being implemented and writes the number of that country, its location, and the reason for the choice.
2. The team brainstorms on the paper ways they can actually help that country.

They are not to edit; they are to write down every idea to keep the ideas flowing.

PUBLISHING

Hang the teams' writings under a banner THE MIND AT WORK WORLDWIDE. Discuss.

Jackdaw 43

BADGES

Fire Prevention Week
(October: The second week)

Title: *Poinsettia and the Firefighters*. Harper & Row, 1984.

Author: Felicia Bond

Jackdaw: A firefighter's badge (available in packages of 30 from school supply stores or American Teaching Aids, see bibliography).

Summary: Poinsettia the Pig feels frightened in her new room until she learns that firefighters stay awake as they keep watch all through the night.

READING/WRITING CONNECTIONS

1. Wear a firefighter's badge while you talk about firefighters. Tell students that on October 8, 1871, Chicago had a fire that destroyed much of the city. Explain that we remember that day during this week so we can keep such a disastrous fire from happening again. Elicit suggestions from students about ways to prevent fires. Students talk about what they should do if there is a fire in school or at home.
2. Allow ample time for students to look at the cover and conjecture about Poinsettia.
3. Discuss times when students have heard strange noises in the night. Ask students to speculate why Poinsettia was no longer afraid at the end of the book. Discuss safety around wires.
4. Distribute firefighters' badges. Students draw or write their favorite part of the story.
5. Hang a long sheet of butcher paper across a wall. Students share the story part they chose and why they liked it. Then they tape it in the correct sequence of the story—beginning, middle, end. If no one has chosen an important part, together write it in the correct place.

—EXTENSIONS—

LIBRARY CONNECTIONS

1. Extend fire safety to other kinds of safety through Marc Brown and Stephen Krensky's *Dinosaurs, Beware! A Safety Guide*. Especially stress the fire safety rules.
2. Work in small groups to create bookmarks that list two or three safety rules. Share the bookmarks with students and staff.

INTEGRATED ACTIVITY

1. Students construct tissue paper firescapes. a. Draw telephone wires on blue cardboard or a house on white cardboard. b. Tear pieces of tissue paper into pieces that look like tongues of fire. c. Brush white glue on the cardboard around the wires or house. d. Put the tissue paper on the glue to look like a fire.
2. Write a "how to prevent a fire" paper. Staple to the tissue art.

PUBLISHING

Students sit in a SAFETY CIRCLE. Students read their papers and show their tissue art. Display.

Jackdaw 44

LOCKED LOGBOOKS

Columbus Day
(October 12—Often observed the second Monday of October)

Title: *Follow the Dream: The Story of Christopher Columbus*. Alfred A. Knopf, 1991.
Author: Peter Sis
Jackdaw: A locked logbook.
Summary: A pictorial retelling of Columbus's story. It shows how he overcame obstacles to fulfill his dream of sailing west in an attempt to find a new route to the Orient.

READING/WRITING CONNECTIONS

1. Show the dust jacket. Discuss the strange objects surrounding the boat. Show the cover. Speculate why Sis would show three boats so microscopically. Read and discuss the author information.
2. As you read and show the book, point out how its art extends its meaning.
3. Make Columbus logbooks: a. Fold 8-½″ x 11″ paper in half, short side to short side. b. Fold a one-inch flap on top and bottom. c. On the top flap, measure 2″ in from each side and mark. d. Cut in toward marks to form tabs. Crease tabs in. e. On the other flap, cut along fold in the middle to form a slit, leaving about 2″ on either side. f. Insert tabs in slit and crease to make a locked book that measures 5-½″ x 3-¼″.
4. Have students extend the pictured logs from the book into elaborated written log entries. Share.

—EXTENSIONS—

LIBRARY CONNECTIONS

1. In "A Note to the Reader," Sis talks about the book's endpapers. Examine these endpapers and endpapers in other books, including some older books. Discuss how contemporary books use endpapers functionally. Stress the importance of all parts of a book.
2. Distribute different colored paper the size of the book's endpapers. Divide students into groups. Using atlases, maps, globes, and historical references, each group designs different endpapers that integrate with the book's meaning. Students show and explain their designs and color choices.

INTEGRATED ACTIVITY

1. Columbus used a telescope on his voyage. Help students perform this experiment: a. In a darkened room, students close one eye and look out an open window through a magnifying lens. They adjust the lens back and forth until an object comes into focus. b. They write results (upside-down image). c. Students place a second lens between themselves and the first lens and move it back and forth until the image is clear. d. They write results (image remains upside down but is larger). They speculate on the reasons for these results (refracting telescopes).
2. Research what is added to give terrestrial telescopes an upright view (an extra convex lens), lenses, and the reflecting telescope. Use Macaulay's *The Way Things Work*.

PUBLISHING

Create a COLUMBUS DAY bulletin board out of brown paper bags that have been moistened and dried (this gives a weathered, textured quality). Display students' logbooks.

Jackdaw 45

NATURE PICTURES

National Poetry Day
(October 15)

Title: *Seasons*. Doubleday, 1990.

Author: Warabe Aska, poetry selected by Alberto Manguel

Jackdaw: A nature picture.

Summary: The four seasons are captured through art and poetry.

READING/WRITING CONNECTIONS

1. Inform students that today is National Poetry Day because Virgil, the Roman poet, was born on this day in 70 B.C. Tell them Virgil wrote the *Aeneid*, considered one of the greatest epic poems in world literature. It tells the story of Aeneas, a Trojan, son of Anchises and Venus, who, after Troy's fall, escapes to Italy. His descendants are credited with founding Rome, while Virgil is credited with influencing all poets who came after him.

2. In honor of the day, explain that the class will together share and experience some poetry. Discuss how people generally feel about poetry and why and students' own experiences with poetry.

3. Read Larkin's poem "The Trees" and study the picture on the title page. Discuss. Read the introduction. Then turn to page 19 and see if the students can meet Aska's challenge.

4. Choose among the selections. Discuss the figurative language appropriate for the class.

5. Distribute nature pictures and invite students to write a poem to accompany their picture. Share.

—EXTENSIONS—

LIBRARY CONNECTIONS

Share and display other poetry books with students: Paul B. Janeczko's *Brickyard Summer* contains poems of people, places, and events through the eyes of remembered adolescence; Gary Soto's *A Fire In My Hands* captures his early life poetically; Charles Sullivan's *Imaginary Gardens: American Poetry and Art for Young People* provides all the classics side-by-side with great art; e.e. cumming's *in Just-spring* moves the delightful poem into a delightful picture book; David Woolger's *Who do you think you are? Poems About People* runs the gamut of types of people, poems, and emotions; Valerie Worth's *all the small poems* uses common objects uncommonly; Jack Prelutsky's *For Laughing Out Loud: Poems to Tickle Your Funnybone* does just that.

INTEGRATED ACTIVITY

1. Let students, working in pairs, choose a poem from Theoni Pappas's *Math Talk: Mathematical Ideas in Poems for Two Voices* to present to the class.

2. Challenge students to take a mathematical concept and write it up as a poem for two voices, using Pappas's poems as a model.

PUBLISHING

Students present their readings of Pappas's poems and their original work.

JACKDAW 45—Copyright 1992 Teacher Ideas Press, a division of Libraries Unlimited, Inc., P.O. Box 6633, Englewood, CO 80155-6633

Jackdaw 46

MATCHBOXES

United Nations Day
(October 24)

Title: *Angel Child, Dragon Child*. Scholastic, 1989.
Author: Michele Maria Surat
Jackdaw: A matchbox.
Summary: Ut struggles to adapt following her move from Vietnam to America.

READING/WRITING CONNECTIONS

1. Before you begin this book, take pictures of students to put in empty matchboxes.
2. Distribute the matchboxes at random. Explain that today we honor the United Nations, an international organization established immediately after World War II to promote and maintain peace, security, and cooperation among all nations. Discuss recent news involving the United Nations and how U.N. delegates must work to understand the culture, history, and motivations of delegates from other countries. Use this discussion to introduce the book.
3. After reading the book, invite students to open their matchbooks, find the person pictured, and talk to that person about the book: their favorite parts, their favorite characters, their feelings, recommendations, surprises, and other similar topics. After this experience, students write on an index card what they learned about other people from the book and from discussing the book with another person. Share.

—EXTENSIONS—

LIBRARY CONNECTIONS

1. Send a postcard for a United Nations Teacher's Kit, United Nations Public Inquiries Unit, Room GA-57, United Nations, New York, NY 10017.
2. Divide students into five groups to research: U.N. member countries; the U.N. flag; the year Vietnam became a member of the United Nations; the names and functions of the six bodies designated by the U.N. charter; and UNICEF.
3. Groups present their results through video, tapes, pictures, dramatizations, puppets, or other multimedia forms.

INTEGRATED ACTIVITY

1. Begin by explaining that the United Nations Building is based on the principle of the golden rectangle. Give students a construction paper rectangle that measures 8" x 13". After students measure its length and width, they find the ratio of the length to the width (which should be close to .618 to 1, the golden ratio).
2. Using calculators, students compare that ratio to 3" x 5" index cards, paperback books, the length from the top of the head to the navel and the length from the navel to the toes.
3. Culminate the activity by watching *Donald Duck in Math Magic Land*, produced by Walt Disney Productions, available in most video stores.

PUBLISHING

Invite a person from another country to speak to the students and to view their work.

JACKDAW 46—Copyright 1992 Teacher Ideas Press, a division of Libraries Unlimited, Inc., P.O. Box 6633, Englewood, CO 80155-6633

Jackdaw 47

MASKS

Halloween
(October 31)

Title: *That Terrible Halloween Night*. Mulberry Books, 1980.
Author: James Stevenson
Jackdaw: A mask.
Summary: Grandpa tells Mary Ann and Louie about a terrible Halloween night that turned him into an old man.

READING/WRITING CONNECTIONS

1. Introduce the book by telling students that *hallowed* means holy and that *een* is a shortened version of *evening*. For centuries people believed that Halloween was the night dead spirits roamed. Therefore, they dressed in costumes to fool or frighten these spirits. Ask students to tell about their Halloween customs. Ask if they ever tried to scare someone and it did not work or the tables were turned on them. Discuss. Talk about why we might want to scare someone, how it feels to scare someone, and how it feels to be scared.
2. Read the book; stop to invite predictions. Discuss Grandpa's expression on the last page.
3. Engage students in making corrugated-paper masks. Students bend the cardboard around their faces, make holes on each side for elastic to hold it on, cut holes for eyes, and decorate the faces, using the corrugated texture for effect.

—EXTENSIONS—

LIBRARY CONNECTIONS

1. Share books with students on the Celtic people of the British Isles, who celebrated harvest festivals corresponding to Halloween.
2. Display masks from around the world, books about masks, or both. Speculate on the purposes of masks.

INTEGRATED ACTIVITY

When Grandpa asks the creature who it is, it answers, "I am the worst parts of a lot of things...." By playing with that line, students not only elaborate on the answer, but also begin to develop logical connections by laying the foundation for syllogistic thought patterns. Divide students into pairs. **A** begins by writing, "The worst part of _____ is _____." **B** follows by using the last words of **A**'s statement, and so on. For example,

    A: The worst part of the dentist is going.
    B: The worst part of going is looking at the drill.
    A: The worst part of the drill ... and so on.

(In defense of dentists, they might conclude: "The best part ... is healthy teeth!") Share.

PUBLISHING

Make a large purple-striped door out of cardboard. Hang students' work behind the door.

Jackdaw 48

FOLD-OUTS

NOVEMBER
American Art Week
(November: The first week)

Title: *Ah!* Harry N. Abrams, 1992.

Author: Josse Goffin

Jackdaw: A large (25" x 10") piece of quality paper.

Summary: This book stimulates the imagination while introducing 12 artistic masterpieces.

READING/WRITING CONNECTIONS

1. Write the word *Ah* on the board. Ask students if they know that the word is called an interjection. Brainstorm the feelings that would evoke the expression "Ah!" (surprise, joy, appreciation, pity, understanding, and so forth).
2. Show the book's cover. Invite predictions about the nature of the book, what kind of book it might be, and its purpose. Ask if anyone recognizes the author.
3. Open to the hat. Invite more speculation about the book. Ask students to tell you what is there and what is not there. Open the flap. Discuss the painting. Check if anyone notices the wooden shoe.
4. Open to the wooden shoe. Continue in this way through all fold-out pages and 12 paintings. The "Ah" will come to students at different times, as a cumulative effect takes place.
5. Quickly divide students into AH (idea) GROUPS of two or three. Using the book as a model, each group designs a page, pencil sketches on paper, and decides on an art masterpiece (have art books available) to display as part of a fold-out page. Share ideas. Conclude by informing students that this is the beginning of American Art Week. By the end of the week, each group should have its fold-out page (and the answer square for the back cover) complete for a class AH ART book.

—EXTENSIONS—

LIBRARY CONNECTIONS

1. Share and display other books about art. See Carroll's *Story Books*, Jackdaw 27. Invite students to feel comfortable browsing through them. Discuss art and books about art.
2. Show students the art section of the library.
3. Have students create a bibliography of art books that prompt an "Ah!"

INTEGRATED ACTIVITY

1. Working in small groups, students choose one of the paintings in the book to thoroughly research: the artist, the country of origin, the artistic period, historical occurrences of the time, and any stories, legends, or controversies associated with that particular piece of art.
2. Arrange for groups to present their findings through video, tapes, pictures, dramatizations, or puppets.

PUBLISHING
Share the finished fold-out pages. Bind and display with other art books under an AH! banner.

JACKDAW 48—Copyright 1992 Teacher Ideas Press, a division of Libraries Unlimited, Inc., P.O. Box 6633, Englewood, CO 80155-6633

Jackdaw 49

MEDALS

Veterans' Day
(November 11)

Title: *My Daddy Was a Soldier: A World War II Story.* Holiday House, 1990.

Author: Deborah Kogan Ray

Jackdaw: A gold paper medal.

Summary: Jeannie-o recounts her memories during the time her daddy served in the Pacific during World War II.

READING/WRITING CONNECTIONS

1. Write *veteran* and *war* on the board. Discuss. Explain that Veterans' Day, originally called Armistice Day, commemorated the day in 1918 when an armistice was declared between the Central and Allied powers ending World War I. In 1954, the United States changed the name to extend the honor to everyone who had served in any U.S. war.
2. After reading the book, talk about the feelings it generated. Ask students if the cover captures the beginning or end of the book. Ask for reasons for their responses.
3. Distribute medals. Students write as if they are veterans. They are to identify the war in which they served and the reason they were awarded their commendations. Share.

—EXTENSIONS—

LIBRARY CONNECTIONS

1. Using maps, globes, and atlases, help students locate the places referred to in the book, such as Pearl Harbor in Hawaii, England, San Diego, the Pacific, Italy, and Chicago.
2. Using cash register tape, students create a time line banner beginning with December 7, 1941, when the book begins, and ending with December, 1945, when Daddy comes home. Using library resources, they research events that occurred during this time and add them to the banner.
3. Create a sensory experience day: Turn off all the lights and talk about blackouts. Play an old radio program (available on tapes). Prepare individual cups of cornflakes sprinkled with corn syrup for tasting. Show a ration book. Explain how these worked when buying food or gas. Distribute pictures of service members in uniform for students to examine. Play a tape of an air-raid siren. Cut tiny pieces of Spam for tasting.

INTEGRATED ACTIVITY

1. Show the Academy Award-winning film (seven Oscars) *The Best Years of Our Lives* (available from most video stores under the category "classic films"), which examines the problems of three World War II servicemen trying to readjust to peacetime.
2. After the film, students write their reactions to the adjustments of the sergeant, the sailor who lost both his hands, and the Air Force officer.

PUBLISHING

Share reactions to the film in a VETERAN'S DAY read-around.

JACKDAW 49—Copyright 1992 Teacher Ideas Press, a division of Libraries Unlimited, Inc., P.O. Box 6633, Englewood, CO 80155-6633

Jackdaw 50 — BOOKS

National Children's Book Week
(November: Third week)

Title: *How a Book Is Made*. Harper & Row, 1986.
Author: Aliki
Jackdaw: A book.
Summary: This book describes the steps involved in making a book: the people involved; writing and illustrating; the technical processes needed to print a book; and publishing, selling, and buying. It concludes with owning a book.

READING/WRITING CONNECTIONS

1. Divide students into groups of four or five. Assign a scribe for each group. Ask students to list the steps they think goes into making a book. Groups share their lists.
2. After reading the book, have students return to their lists, add any steps mentioned in the book that were not suggested, and delete any extraneous steps. Discuss.
3. Ask students to choose from among their prewritings a piece to polish for a book. They also decide on a size and color for the book.
4. Help each student make a book: a. Cut cardboard covers one-half inch larger than the paper used for the story; b. Place the pages for the story between these two covers; c. Clip all around to firmly hold pages and covers in place; d. Measure and mark every quarter inch along the binding side of the front cover; e. Poke a hole through the covers and pages at the quarter-inch intervals; f. Sew through these holes with dental floss; g. Cover stitches with colorful tape.
5. Have students, working in groups, construct a list of steps telling how they made their books. Compare these to the first lists. Discuss.

—EXTENSIONS—

LIBRARY CONNECTIONS

1. Use the title page to review the parts of the book from title page, title, copyright page, to spine, gutter, publisher, author (and illustrator), and back flap.
2. Choose from among the library holdings a variety of books. Examine their parts. Draw conclusions. Share the note on the copyright page that explains and validates how the making of a book can vary from publishing house to publishing house.

INTEGRATED ACTIVITY

Students complete their books by writing and illustrating the final copy. They write the title and author on the front cover and "About the Author" on the back cover. The librarian may bring library pockets for students to complete and affix in the books so they may be checked out.

PUBLISHING

Display books on a bulletin board entitled NATIONAL CHILDREN'S BOOK WEEK.

JACKDAW 50—Copyright 1992 Teacher Ideas Press, a division of Libraries Unlimited, Inc., P.O. Box 6633, Englewood, CO 80155-6633

Jackdaw 51

DRIED FRUIT

Thanksgiving Day
(November: Fourth Thursday)

Title: *N. C. Wyeth's Pilgrims*. Chronicle Books, 1991.

Author: Robert San Souci

Jackdaw: A piece of dried fruit.

Summary: This book recounts the story of the coming of the Pilgrims to America. The illustrations by N. C. Wyeth were originally commissioned by the Metropolitan Life Insurance Company as murals.

READING/WRITING CONNECTIONS

1. Discuss Thanksgiving. Draw from students' previous knowledge information about this American holiday. Share additional information from the "Author's Note."
2. Read the book. Take time for students to savor Wyeth's rich illustrations.
3. Distribute pieces of dried fruit. Invite students to write how they might feel if they were a Separatist, a Stranger, or an Indian in Plymouth during April 1621 as the *Mayflower* embarked on its return voyage to England. Share.

—EXTENSIONS—

LIBRARY CONNECTIONS

1. The endpapers are copies of the Mayflower's original passenger list. Read. Count the numbers and discuss the information and the writing style.
2. Extend students' background of the Wyeths by reading and showing appropriate selections from Richard Meryman's *First Impressions: Andrew Wyeth*.

INTEGRATED ACTIVITY

1. This book provides an excellent introduction to the colonial period of American literature. Older students may research the period using sources such as Bradford Smith's biography of William Bradford, *Bradford of Plymouth*; William Bradford's *Mourt's Relation*, which contains a letter colonist Edward Winslow sent to a friend describing the first Thanksgiving in the colonies; William Bradford's *Of Plymouth Plantation: Sixteen Twenty to Sixteen Forty-Seven*, the historical account of the colony, told in what Bradford called "plain style" (to distinguish from the English notion of "high style" writing); and Thomas J. Fleming's *One Small Candle: The Pilgrims' First Year in America*, a detailed account of the first Thanksgiving.
2. Write the researched information in an interesting manner, as if for a book or journal.
3. Using parchment paper or ecru-colored paper, students construct a corn-husk cover for their researched information. Lightly draw an outline of a corn cob. Use fingers and thumbs dipped in orange, yellow, red, and blue tempera paint to make print kernels. Glue dried corn husks (or crepe paper) around kernels to resemble an ear of Indian corn.

PUBLISHING

In a Thanksgiving Day read-around, each student shares a page from his or her corn-husk book. Complete the reading with a Thanksgiving celebration by eating foods of the period.

JACKDAW 51—Copyright 1992 Teacher Ideas Press, a division of Libraries Unlimited, Inc., P.O. Box 6633, Englewood, CO 80155-6633

Jackdaw 52

TURTLE OUTLINES

Indian Heritage Day
(November 25)

Title: *Thirteen Moons on Turtle's Back: A Native American Year of Moons*. Philomel Books, 1992.

Authors: Joseph Bruchac and Jonathan London

Jackdaw: An outline of a turtle like the one opposite the dedication page.

Summary: Uses poems based on Native American legends to celebrate the seasons.

READING/WRITING CONNECTIONS

1. Bring a live turtle, turtle figurine, or turtle shell to class. Examine its back. Count its scales. Explain that many Native American cultures believe that each of the scales holds a story of the season. They called the seasons *moons*. Inform students that this is Indian Heritage Day, a day when we celebrate and appreciate all the things we have inherited from Native Americans.

2. Brainstorm what we have inherited from Native Americans, including items and words such as corn, toboggan, teepee, raccoon, hominy, hickory, moccasin, beans, chile, squash, succotash, and so forth. Lead students to understand that the greatest gift we have received from Native Americans is their respect for the balance and connectedness of nature.

3. Read "A note about this book." Discuss. Read the introductory page. Allow time for students to savor Thomas Locker's illustrations. Then choose several poems to read and discuss.

4. Let each student pick a number from 1 to 13. Distribute the turtle outlines. Ask students to use the numbers they picked as the number of their moon and write a poem or story related to that season. Share.

—EXTENSIONS—

LIBRARY CONNECTIONS

Read "It All Began with Indian Corn" from Lila Perl's *Slumps, Grunts, and Snickerdoodles: What Colonial America Ate and Why* or Aliki's *Corn Is Maize: The Gift of the Indians*. Discuss.

INTEGRATED ACTIVITY

Divide students into pairs. Each pair researches one of the 13 Native American tribal nations represented in the book. Partners must include in their research: 1. A map showing the original area of this nation. 2. A description of their way of life. 3. An example of their respect for nature. 4. Something they contributed to our civilization. 5. A rendition of the poem representative of that nation from the book, recreated either on video, audiotape, or through some type of dramatization.

PUBLISHING

Celebrate NATIVE AMERICAN HERITAGE DAY with an Indian feast. Use Suzanne Barchers's *Cooking Up U.S. History: Recipes and Research to Share with Children*. Ask for volunteers to bring in various dishes such as roasted nuts, popcorn balls, hominy, and so forth.

JACKDAW 52—Copyright 1992 Teacher Ideas Press, a division of Libraries Unlimited, Inc., P.O. Box 6633, Englewood, CO 80155-6633

Jackdaw 53

COOKIES

DECEMBER
St. Nicholas Day
(December 6)

Title: *The Baker's Dozen: A Colonial American Tale*. Harcourt Brace Jovanovich, 1988.

Author: Heather Forest

Jackdaw: A St. Nicholas cookie.

Summary: A mysterious old woman and a St. Nicholas cookie teach a greedy baker a lesson.

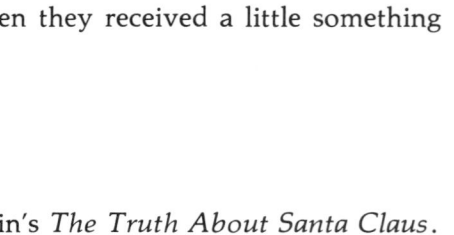

READING/WRITING CONNECTIONS

1. Elicit from students what they know about St. Nicholas. Speculate how and why a real person, a Byzantine bishop of the fourth century, would still be celebrated. Show students where he was born (Turkey) on a map or globe. Known for his kindness, he is especially honored in Holland, France, and Belgium and is associated with the giving of sweets.

2. Show the book jacket. Ask students if they know the expression "a baker's dozen." Discuss how people were once fined for giving short weights, so bakers threw in another loaf to make certain the weight was proper. This was called "vantage loaf" and became a custom. Read the "Author's Note" as an introduction.

3. Distribute the St. Nicholas cookies. Students write about a time when they received a little something extra. Share.

—EXTENSIONS—

LIBRARY CONNECTIONS

1. Share with students the history of St. Nicholas. Use James Cross Giblin's *The Truth About Santa Claus*.

2. Read the reproduction of Clement Clarke Moore's *The Night Before Christmas or a Visit of St. Nicholas*. The introduction by Dr. Russell Barber provides a reliable history of this classic.

INTEGRATED ACTIVITY

1. Divide students into groups of three. Students brainstorm items that could appropriately be purchased by the dozen, with a thirteenth item "thrown in." For example, shoes would not be appropriately purchased by the dozen, but flowers would.

2. After the lists have been generated, share lists.

3. After sharing, students circle one item on their own list they decide is most apt.

4. Assign the chosen items a reasonable wholesale price per item, a wholesale price per dozen, a retail price per item, and a retail price per dozen.

5. Calculate the profit for the seller based on a dozen and the profit based on a baker's dozen. Discuss the advantages and disadvantages of giving a baker's dozen.

6. On butcher paper, draw their items, graph the calculations, and write out how they determined the profit.

PUBLISHING

Share results of the mathematics activity and post the results.

JACKDAW 53—Copyright 1992 Teacher Ideas Press, a division of Libraries Unlimited, Inc., P.O. Box 6633, Englewood, CO 80155-6633

Jackdaw 54

PASTEL PAGES

Winter Solstice
(December 21 or 22)

Title: *Goodbye Geese*. Philomel Books, 1991.

Author: Nancy White Carlstrom

Jackdaw: A pastel drawing of winter.

Summary: A child asks questions about winter as if winter were a woman. The father answers each question using poetic imagery.

READING/WRITING CONNECTIONS

1. Introduce the book by asking students to personify winter by writing one question to winter as if the season were a person. Collect the questions.
2. Read the book. Provide ample time to discuss the poetry and illustrations.
3. Redistribute the questions so no student receives his or her own question. Using the book as a model, invite students to write a response to the questions they were given.
4. On drawing paper, again using the book as model, each student prints the question and the answer and creates an appropriate image with pastels to complete the page. Share.

—EXTENSIONS—

LIBRARY CONNECTIONS

The illustrations were done by Caldecott-winning artist Ed Young. Create a display of other books written and illustrated by Young, such as *Lon Po Po*. Compare his illustrations. Discuss the variations as related to the story, mood, setting, etc.

INTEGRATED ACTIVITY

1. Explain the winter solstice. On a world globe, locate a point in the United States. Darken the room. With a strong flashlight, show how during this time of the year the earth is tilted away from the sun as it goes around the sun. Therefore, the winter solstice is the shortest day and longest night of the year.
2. Perform this experiment:
   a. Place one sheet of carbon paper, carbon side down, over one sheet of typing paper under the clip on a clipboard.
   b. Affix a small hunk of modeling clay under each corner of the clip end of the board.
   c. Lay an empty paper towel tube horizontally across the halfway point of the papers.
   d. Elevate the end of the tube off the board with another hunk of clay.
   e. Put a marble into the elevated end of the tube and allow it to roll out and down.
   f. Look at the pattern the marble left by raising the carbon paper.
3. Have students write up the results of this experiment and make connections between the results and the winter solstice. (Adapted from Janice VanCleave's *Astronomy for Every Kid*.)

PUBLISHING

Display the questions, answers, and drawings of students on a WINTER MYSTERIES bulletin board.

JACKDAW 54—Copyright 1992 Teacher Ideas Press, a division of Libraries Unlimited, Inc., P.O. Box 6633, Englewood, CO 80155-6633

Jackdaw 55

CANDLES

Hanukkah
(December: Eight days beginning on the 25th day of the Hebrew month Kislev)

Title: *Hershel and the Hanukkah Goblins*. Holiday House, 1985.
Author: Eric Kimmel
Jackdaw: A tiny *shammes* (servant) candle.
Summary: This folktale relates how Hershel outsmarts goblins who haunt the old synagogue, so that the townspeople may again celebrate Hanukkah.

READING/WRITING CONNECTIONS

1. Explain that the word *Hanukkah* means "dedication." Invite students to tell what they know about this holiday. Some may offer information about the songs sung, the little presents exchanged, or the games played. Show a menorah. Describe how the Jewish people use this candelabrum to recall their triumph over the Syrian king Antiochus IV in 165 B.C. After Judah Maccabee conquered the king, the Jews wanted to rededicate their Temple, but they had only enough oil to burn for one day. Miraculously, the oil lasted eight days. That is why the menorah holds eight candles.

2. Distribute the *shammes* candles. Show how the candles in the menorah are lit with this extra "servant" candle.

3. After reading the book, talk about the ways Hershel outsmarted the goblins on the first, second, third, and last night of Hanukkah. Then divide students into small groups. Explain that each group is to write one way Hershel may have outsmarted the goblins on the fourth, fifth, or sixth nights. Read Kimmel's commentary at the end of the book to provide more information for students to use. Share.

—EXTENSIONS—

LIBRARY CONNECTIONS

1. This book is a Caldecott Honor Book. Show Trina Schart Hyman's other Caldecott Medal winners: *Saint George and the Dragon* and *Little Red Riding Hood*. Discuss her art style.

2. Help students comb the library for other Caldecott winners. Display a sampling of Caldecott and non-Caldecott books. Invite students to examine both and come up with criteria that might be used to decide which books receive the award. Share reviews from *The Hornbook*. Do students agree with the reviews?

INTEGRATED ACTIVITY

1. The reader only sees the outline of the King of the Goblins, yet Hershel grows faint when he looks at it. Speculate why Kimmel did not give a detailed illustration of this character. Look at Hershel's expression when he sees it. Review the words used to describe it.

2. Encourage students to draw their rendition of the King of the Goblins.

3. Exchange drawings and write a detailed description of the character. Give it a name.

PUBLISHING

Celebrate a HAPPY HANUKKAH read-around with the eating of potato latkes and the sharing of drawings and descriptions of the King of the Goblins whom Hershel outsmarted.

JACKDAW 55—Copyright 1992 Teacher Ideas Press, a division of Libraries Unlimited, Inc., P.O. Box 6633, Englewood, CO 80155-6633

Jackdaw 56

RINGS

Christmas
(December 25)

Title: *Emma's Christmas*. Orchard Books, 1988.

Author: Irene Trivas

Jackdaw: A wedding ring (see bibliography; available in packages of 144 from U.S. Toy Company).

Summary: Emma, a country girl, is courted by a prince who gives her the gifts of the 12 days of Christmas.

READING/WRITING CONNECTIONS

1. Play any one of the numerous renditions of the carol "The Twelve Days of Christmas." Tell students to listen carefully to each of the gifts. Afterwards, ask students to recall the gifts and their numbers. Write these on the board. Check for accuracy. Invite conjecture about what would happen as these gifts accumulated.

2. After discussing conjectures, explain that is just what happens in *Emma's Christmas*. Before reading, caution students to listen carefully to all the gifts and their numbers. Add together all the gifts at Emma's on the twelfth day (376, including the pear trees but not the bride and groom).

3. Distribute the gold rings and index cards. Ask, "If Emma had 40 golden rings on the twelfth day of Christmas, as the book states, how many would she have if she continued to receive five a day until New Year's Day?" Students do the computation on one side of the card and write the explanation of how they did it on the reverse side. Share.

—EXTENSIONS—

LIBRARY CONNECTIONS

1. Read Manghanita Kempadoo's *Letters of Thanks: A Christmas Tale*, which provides insight into the recipient's reactions as conveyed through her letters. Students, working in groups, compose a letter for the gifts of a day of their choice, using this book as a model. Share.

2. Divide students into groups. Each group devises 12 days of contemporary gifts that might be sent to one's true love this Christmas. Share.

INTEGRATED ACTIVITY

Divide students into three groups. Group I composes a rap version of "The Twelve Days of Christmas." Provide Ann Baker and Johnny Baker's *Raps & Rhymes in Math* for a model. Group II analyzes the story for the different geometric shapes of the gifts. They are to prepare a mathematical way to present their findings. Group III calculates the number of gifts Emma would have received had she kept the prince waiting until Valentine's Day or until the following Christmas. Based on those calculations, the group composes a different ending.

PUBLISHING

Students sit in a circle to share their findings. Conclude by singing "The Twelve Days of Christmas."

Jackdaw 57

BOXES

Boxing Day
(December 26)

Title: *The Jolly Christmas Postman*. Little, Brown & Co., 1991.
Authors: Janet Ahlberg and Allan Ahlberg
Jackdaw: An origami box.
Summary: A jolly postman delivers mail on Christmas Eve to fairy-tale characters.

READING/WRITING CONNECTIONS

1. Show *The Jolly Postman or Other People's Letters*. Ask students to tell what they remember about the book. Then show the Christmas version. Invite predictions on how this version might be similar to or different from the original.
2. Read the book. Take time to share in detail each piece of mail.
3. After the reading, discuss how the postman must feel. Talk about how people express their appreciation to postal carriers and others who perform services for them. Explain that in Canada, England, and several other countries, people honor a tradition dating back about 100 years by setting aside December 26 as a time for giving Christmas boxes to these people. Discuss other gift-giving traditions.
4. Allow each student to make two origami boxes. Use papers and instructions from Yasutomo & Co., Brisbane, CA 94005 (available in most craft stores) or any good origami instruction book. The boxes should fit one inside the other to form a top and bottom. Students decorate their box.
5. Divide students into small groups. Groups brainstorm what they would write to a postal carrier or other service person to put inside their boxes. Suggest that students think of specific, special things that can be referenced. Each student writes something. All share.

—EXTENSIONS—

LIBRARY CONNECTIONS

1. Divide students into six small groups: the Christmas Joke group; the Christmas Game group; the Christmas Jigsaw Puzzle group; the Christmas Book group; the Christmas Guide group; the Christmas Card group. Each group chooses a character in literature.
2. Give each group the contents of one envelope from the book to use as a model. Students create an appropriate version of their model to be sent to their chosen character. Share.

INTEGRATED ACTIVITY

1. Divide students into groups of three. Each group cuts five 3" squares from lightweight cardboard. Challenge each group to arrange and rearrange the squares in 12 different ways so that their edges touch and their corners line up. Then they draw and cut out each arrangement.
2. Let students experiment to find which arrangements can be folded up into boxes.

PUBLISHING

Create a BOXING DAY display. Arrange students' boxes around the book. Laminate an explanation of this tradition to add to the display.

Jackdaw 58

WOVEN MATS

DECEMBER/JANUARY
Kwanzaa
(December 26-January 1)

Title: *Kwanzaa*. Children's Press, 1990.

Author: Deborah M. Newton Chocolate

Jackdaw: A woven mat.

Summary: The story portrays the celebration of Kwanzaa, an African-American holiday. The narrator takes the reader through the seven-day celebration with his family.

READING/WRITING CONNECTIONS

1. Distribute to each student one neon-colored piece of cover stock and one brightly-colored piece of paper. Instruct students in mat making: a. Fold the cover stock in half, short end to short end. b. Draw lines, one inch apart, from the fold to one inch from the paper's edge. c. Open and spread flat. This serves as a paper "loom." d. Cut one-inch strips from the paper. e. Weave each strip into the loom. f. Tape the edges of each strip as you go. g. Glue the entire mat onto a larger piece of paper (students choose color). h. Label the mat *MKEKE*.

2. Explain that the mat is one of the symbols of Kwanzaa. It represents reverence for tradition. This seven-day holiday is the time African-Americans celebrate community ties and unity of the family and reestablish links to an African past. Inform students that this cultural observance was begun in 1966 for African-Americans by Maulana Karenga, a professor at California State University. Karenga synthesized many elements from African harvest festivals to create this celebration. Read the introduction. Discuss.

3. After reading the book, invite students to write on the back of the mat a tradition they observe as part of their cultural heritage or a tradition they observe on a holiday or as a family. Share. Laminate mats for display.

—EXTENSIONS—

LIBRARY CONNECTIONS

Share Eric V. Copage's book *Kwanzaa: An African-American Celebration of Culture and Cooking*. Show the endpages, a weaving of woven mats, and designs. Read several recipes, for example, "Kiddie (Goat) Stew" (page 109). Use this book to teach the parts of a book, because it is so extensive.

INTEGRATED ACTIVITY

Celebrate each of the seven days of Kwanzaa with seven groups. Each group takes a day and plans it for the class, using the appropriate principle of Kwanzaa: Day 1, unity; Day 2, self-determination; Day 3, collective work and responsibility; Day 4, cooperative economics; Day 5, purpose; Day 6, creativity; Day 7, faith. The groups explain the day's principle, introduce Swahili words used, provide an activity or piece of literature that extends the day's principle, and writes an evaluation of its own work.

PUBLISHING

Decorate the room in the colors of Kwanzaa: black, red, and green. Display the mats and the work and art generated throughout the seven days of group-led projects.

BIBLIOGRAPHY

Adams, Barbara Johnston. *The Go-Around Dollar*. New York: Four Winds Press, 1992.
Ahlberg, Janet, and Allan Ahlberg. *The Jolly Christmas Postman*. New York: Little, Brown & Co., 1991; *The Jolly Postman or Other People's Letters*. New York: Little, Brown & Co., 1986.
Aliki. *Corn Is Maize: The Gift of the Indians*. New York: Harper Trophy, 1976; *How a Book Is Made*. New York: Harper & Row, 1986.
Allison, Diane Worfolk. *This Is the Key to the Kingdom*. Boston: Little, Brown & Co., 1992.
American Teaching Aids. 43254 Hiawatha Avenue South, Minneapolis, MN 55406.
Aska, Warabe (with poetry selected by Alberto Manguel). *Seasons*. New York: Doubleday, 1990.

Baker, Ann, and Johnny Baker. *Raps & Rhymes in Math*. Portsmouth, N.H.: Heinemann Educational Books, 1991.
Barbot, Daniel. *A Bicycle for Rosaura*. New York: Kane/Miller, 1991.
Barchers, Suzanne I. *Cooking Up U.S. History: Recipes and Research to Share with Children*. Englewood, Colo.: Libraries Unlimited, 1991.
Bartlett, John. *Familiar Quotations*. Boston: Little, Brown & Co., 1955.
Baynes, Pauline. *How Dog Began*. New York: Henry Holt & Co., 1985.
Behrens, June. *Fiesta! Cinco de Mayo*. Chicago: Childrens Press, 1978.
Bond, Felicia. *Poinsettia and the Firefighters*. New York: Harper & Row, 1984.
Bosca, Francesca. *Caspar and the Star*. Translated by Philip Hawthorn. Batavia, Ill.: Lion, 1991.
Bradford, William. *Mourt's Relations*. Bedford, Mass.: Applewood Books, 1986; *Of Plymouth Plantation: Sixteen Twenty to Sixteen Forty-Seven*. Edited by Samuel E. Morison. New York: Alfred A. Knopf, 1952.
Breslow, Susan. *I Really Want a Dog*. New York: Dutton Children's Books, 1990.
Brett, Jan. *The First Dog*. New York: Harcourt Brace Jovanovich, 1988.
Bridwell, Norman. *Clifford the Big Red Dog*. New York: Scholastic, 1985.
Brown, Marc. *Arthur's April Fool*. Boston: Little, Brown & Co., 1983.
Brown, Marc, and Stephen Krensky. *Dinosaurs, Beware! A Safety Guide*. Boston: Little, Brown & Co., 1982.
Brown, Ruth. *Our Puppy's Vacation*. New York: E. P. Dutton, 1987.
Bruchac, Joseph, and Jonathan London. *Thirteen Moons on Turtle's Back: A Native American Year of Moons*. New York: Philomel Books, 1992.
Bunting, Eve. *The Wall*. New York: Clarion Books, 1990.
Burns, Marilyn. *Math for Smarty Pants*. Boston: Little, Brown & Co., 1982.

Carle, Eric. *The Very Quiet Cricket*. New York: Philomel Books, 1990.
Carlson, Nancy. *Take Time to Relax!* New York: Viking, 1991.
Carlstrom, Nancy White. *Goodbye Geese*. New York: Philomel Books, 1991.
Carolina Biological Supply Co., 2700 York Road, Burlington, NC 27216-9988; 800-334-5551.
Connecticut Valley Biological Supply Co., Valley Road, P.O. Box 326, Southampton, MA 01073; 800-282-7757, 800-628-7748.
National Geographic Educational Services Catalog (National Geographic Society), 17th and M Streets NW, Washington, DC 20036; 202-857-7000; Nasco, 901 Janesville Avenue, Fort Atkinson, WI 53538; 800-558-9595.
Carroll, Joyce Armstrong. *Story Books: Integrated Teaching of Reading, Writing, Listening, Speaking, Viewing, and Thinking*. Englewood, Colo.: Libraries Unlimited, 1992.
Cherry, Lynne. *A River Ran Wild*. New York: Harcourt Brace Jovanovich, 1992.
Chocolate, Deborah M. Newton. *Kwanzaa*. Chicago: Childrens Press, 1990.
Collins, Judy. *My Father*. Boston: Little, Brown & Co., 1968.
Copage, Eric V. *Kwanzaa: An African-American Celebration of Culture and Cooking*. New York: William Morrow & Co., 1991.
cummings, e. e. *in Just-spring*. Boston: Little, Brown & Co., 1976 (text copyright), 1988 (illustrations copyright).

Day, Alexandra. *Carl's Christmas*. New York: Farrar Straus & Giroux, 1990.
Deedy, Carmen Agra. *Agatha's Feather Bed: Not Just Another Wild Goose Story*. Atlanta, Ga.: Peachtree, 1991.
dePaola, Tomie. *Jamie O'Rourke and the Big Potato*. New York: G. P. Putnam's Sons, 1992.
Donald Duck in Math Magic Land. 27 min. 1959. Disney Productions.
Drucker, Malka, and Rita Pocock. *A Jewish Holiday A B C*. New York: Harcourt Brace Jovanovich, 1992.

Flack, Jerry D. *Inventing, Inventions, and Inventors: A Teaching Resource Book*. Englewood, Colo.: Libraries Unlimited, 1989.

Fleming, Thomas J. *One Small Candle: The Pilgrims' First Year in America*. New York: W. W. Norton, 1964.
Foreman, Michael. *One World*. New York: Arcade, 1990.
Forest, Heather. *The Baker's Dozen: A Colonial American Tale*. New York: Harcourt Brace Jovanovich, 1988.
Fox, Dan, and Claude Marks. *Go In and Out the Window*. New York: Henry Holt & Co., 1987.
Fox, Mem. *Wilfrid Gordon McDonald Partridge*. New York: Kane/Miller, 1985.

Giblin, James Cross. *The Truth About Santa Claus*. New York: Thomas Y. Crowell, 1985.
Giff, Patricia Reilly. *Happy Birthday, Ronald Morgan!* New York: Puffin Books, 1986.
Goffin, Josse. *Ah!* New York: Harry N. Abrams, 1992.
Graham-Barber, Lynda. *Doodle Dandy! The Complete Book of Independence Day Words*. New York: Bradbury Press, 1992.

Horn, Gabriel (White Deer of Autumn). *The Great Change*. Hillsboro, Oreg.: Beyond Words, 1992.
Horton, Zilphia, Frank Hamilton, Guy Carawan, and Pete Seeger. "We Shall Overcome," Ludlow Music, 1963.
Howe, James. *I Wish I Were a Butterfly*. New York: Harcourt Brace Jovanovich, 1987.
Hyman, Trina Schart. *Little Red Riding Hood*. New York: Holiday House, 1983; *Saint George and the Dragon*. Boston: Little, Brown & Co., 1985.

Ikeda, Daisaku. *The Cherry Tree*. New York: Alfred A. Knopf, 1991.

Janeczko, Paul B. *Brickyard Summer*. New York: Orchard Books, 1989.
Joosse, Barbara M. *Mama, Do You Love Me?* San Francisco: Chronicle Books, 1991.

Kaye, Marilyn. *The Real Tooth Fairy*. New York: Harcourt Brace Jovanovich, 1990.
Kempadoo, Manghanita. *Letters of Thanks: A Christmas Tale*. New York: Simon & Schuster, 1969.
Kimmel, Eric. *Hershel and the Hanukkah Goblins*. New York: Holiday House, 1985.
Kovalski, Maryann. *Pizza for Breakfast*. New York: Morrow Junior Books, 1991.
Kroll, Steven. *It's Groundhog Day!* New York: Scholastic, 1987.

Lewis, Paul Owen. *P. Bear's New Year's Party*. Hillsboro, Oreg.: Beyond Words, 1989.
Lopes, Sal. *The Wall: Images and Offerings from the Vietnam Veterans Memorial*. New York: Collins, 1987.
Lyon, George Ella. *A B Cedar: An Alphabet of Trees*. New York: Orchard Books, 1989.

Macaulay, David. *The Way Things Work*. Boston: Houghton Mifflin, 1988.
McElmeel, Sharron L. *Bookpeople: A First Album*. Englewood, Colo.: Libraries Unlimited, 1990.
McLean, Margaret. *Make Your Own Musical Instruments*. Minneapolis, Minn.: Lerner, 1988.
Mendoza, George. *Were You a Wild Duck, Where Would You Go?* New York: Stewart, Tabori & Chang, 1990.
Meryman, Richard. *First Impressions: Andrew Wyeth*. New York: Harry N. Abrams, 1991.
Moore, Clement Clarke. *The Night Before Christmas or a Visit of St. Nicholas*. New York: Philomel Books, 1989.
Morimoto, Junko. *My Hiroshima*. New York: Viking, 1987.
Most, Bernard. *Happy Holidaysaurus!* New York: Harcourt Brace Jovanovich, 1992.
Mudd, Maria M. *The Butterfly*. New York: Stewart, Tabori & Chang, 1991.

Oppenheim, Shulamith Levey. *Appleblossom*. New York: Harcourt Brace Jovanovich, 1991.

Pappas, Theoni. *Math Talk: Mathematical Ideas in Poems for Two Voices*. San Carlos, Cal.: Wide World Publishing/Tetra, 1991.
Perl, Lila. *Slumps, Grunts, and Snickerdoodles: What Colonial America Ate and Why*. New York: Clarion Books, 1975.
Pizer, Abigail. *Nosey Gilbert*. New York: Dial Books for Young Readers, 1987.
Polacco, Patricia. *Rechenka's Eggs*. New York: Philomel Books, 1988.
Prelutsky, Jack, ed. *For Laughing Out Loud: Poems to Tickle Your Funnybone*. New York: Alfred A. Knopf, 1991.
Provensen, Alice. *The Buck Stops Here: The Presidents of the United States*. New York: Harper & Row, 1990.

Ray, Deborah Kogan. *My Daddy Was a Soldier: A World War II Story*. New York: Holiday House, 1990.

San Souci, Robert. *N. C. Wyeth's Pilgrims*. San Francisco: Chronicle Books, 1991.
Schwartz, Amy. *Annabelle Swift, Kindergartner*. New York: Orchard Books, 1988.
Sharmat, Marjorie Weinman. *I'm the Best!* New York: Holiday House, 1991.
Sis, Peter. *Follow the Dream: The Story of Christopher Columbus*. New York: Alfred A. Knopf, 1991.
Smith, Bardford. *Bradford of Plymouth*. New York: J. B. Lippincott, 1951.
Smucker, Anna Egan. *No Star Nights*. New York: Alfred A. Knopf, 1989.
Soto, Gary. *A Fire in My Hands*. Scholastic, 1990.

Copyright 1992 Teacher Ideas Press, a division of Libraries Unlimited, Inc., P.O. Box 6633, Englewood, CO 80155-6633

Spier, Peter. *The Star-Spangled Banner*. New York: Doubleday, 1973.
Spinelli, Eileen. *Somebody Loves You, Mr. Hatch*. New York: Bradbury Press, 1991.
Stafford, William. *The Animal That Drank Up Sound*. New York: Harcourt Brace Jovanovich, 1992.
Stanley, Diane. *Moe the Dog in Tropical Paradise*. G. P. Putnam's Sons, 1992.
Stevenson, James. *That Terrible Halloween Night*. New York: Mulberry Books, 1980.
Sullivan, Charles, ed. *imaginary Gardens: American Poetry and Art for Young People*. New York: Harry N. Abrams, 1989.
Surat, Michele Maria. *Angel Child, Dragon Child*. New York: Scholastic, 1989.

Trivas, Irene. *Emma's Christmas*. New York: Orchard, 1988.

U.S. Toy Company, Inc. 1227 E. 119th St., Grandview, MO 64030 (1-800-255-6124. Fax 816-761-6124).

VanCleave, Janice Pratt. *Astronomy for Every Kid: 101 Easy Experiments That Really Work*. New York: John Wiley & Sons, 1991; *Chemistry for Every Kid: 101 Easy Experiments That Really Work*. New York: John Wiley & Sons, 1989.

Westridge Young Writers Workshop. *Kids Explore America's Hispanic Heritage*. Santa Fe, N.M.: John Muir, 1992.
Wilhelm, Hans. *I'll Always Love You*. New York: Crown, 1985.
Wilson, Edward E. "Autumnal Equinox," in *The Music of What Happens: Poems That Tell Stories*. Selected by Paul B. Janeczko. New York: Orchard Books, 1988.
Woolger, David, ed. *Who do you think you are? Poems About People*. New York: Oxford University Press, 1990.
Worth, Valerie. *all the small poems*. New York: Farrar, Straus & Giroux, 1989.

Xiong, Blia. *Nine-In-One, Grr! Grr!* San Francisco: Children's Book Press, 1989.

Yen, Clara. *Why Rat Comes First: A Story of the Chinese Zodiac*. San Francisco: Children's Book Press, 1991.